P9-CQX-013

Fit
M

THE GREEN
TIGER

THE GREEN TIGER

James FitzGibbon: A Hero of the War of 1812

Enid L. Mallory

McClelland and Stewart

ISBN: 0-7710-5478-5

Maps by Jim Loates

The Canadian Publishers
McClelland and Stewart Limited
25 Hollinger Road, Toronto M4B 3G2

Printed and bound in Canada

To Gord

THE GREEN
TIGER

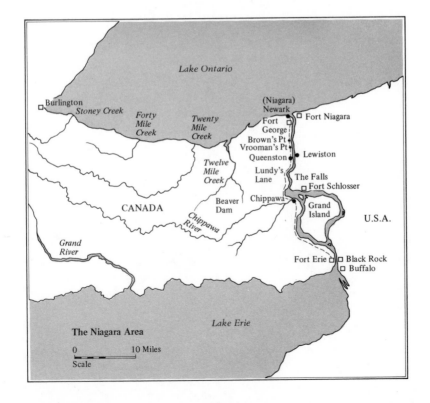

Lake Ontario

Burlington

Stoney Creek

Forty
Mile
Creek

Twenty
Mile
Creek

(Niagara)
Newark

Fort
George

Fort Niagara

Brown's Pt
Vrooman's Pt

Queenston

Lewiston

Twelve
Mile
Creek

Lundy's
Lane

The Falls

Fort Schlosser

CANADA

Beaver
Dam

Chippawa
River

Chippawa

Grand
Island

U.S.A.

Grand
River

Fort Erie

Black Rock

Buffalo

Lake Erie

The Niagara Area

0   10 Miles
Scale

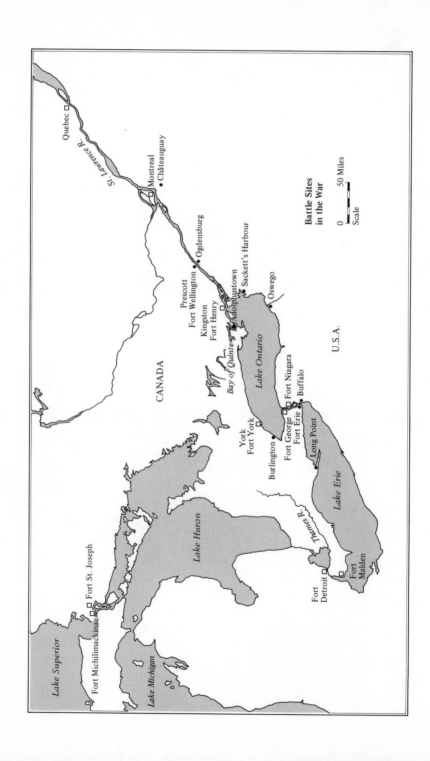

Battle Sites
in the War

0   50 Miles
Scale

Quebec

St. Lawrence R.

Montreal
Châteauguay

Ogdensburg

Prescott
Fort Wellington
Kingston
Fort Henry
Adolphustown
Sackett's Harbour

Oswego

CANADA

Bay of Quinte

Lake Ontario

U.S.A.

Fort Niagara
Buffalo

York
Fort York
Fort George
Fort Erie
Long Point

Burlington

Lake Huron

Thames R.

Lake Erie

Lake Superior

Fort St. Joseph

Fort Michilimackinac

Lake Michigan

Fort
Detroit

Fort
Malden

1

The Irish boy in the cottage by the River Shannon was packing to leave home. The year was 1798. The boy was seventeen, wound up with excitement, and eager to get on to adventure. He had joined the Tarbert Fencibles, a regiment of the British army, and was being sent to do garrison duty in England.

His mother, who was helping him pack, moved with unaccustomed slowness. James could feel her reluctance to let him go. Last night they had talked by candlelight across the family table, and she had wrung a promise from him that he would never enlist for active service abroad. Later, just before he slept, he had heard her extracting the same promise from his captain. He could understand his mother's fears. He had read and heard enough about corporal punishment in the British army; he knew what the lash could do to a man or a boy. He had no intention whatever of volunteering for active service. Going to England would be adventure enough. He fell asleep.

His mother knew him better and she lay awake that night. Her thoughts and memories were a jumble of pride and fear for this, her second son. A great curiosity was in him, a love of ad-

9

venture and an interest in far-away places which made him read every book he could get his hands on. She could remember him struggling to read the *History of Troy's Destruction* because it was the only book the family owned. He was too little to understand most of the words but he kept it hidden in his cot and "read it to pieces," grasping more of it each time. He became known as the best reader in the school, and when other boys had money for a book they would ask James to choose for them. His mother smiled in the night remembering how he always chose one he hadn't read so he could borrow and read it later.

But he was more than a dreamer, this son. He was quick as a cat and just as determined. He was eight years old the day he dragged the big salmon home. Its length was more than he could lift from the ground. He had spied it in the brook by the old castle and leaped in after it, dragged it up the bank and gaffed it with a rusty old knife.

She wondered how her husband could sleep so peacefully with James going away in the morning. When he had enrolled himself, their eldest son John, and this son, James, in the yeomanry corps being formed to defend Ireland against threatened invasion by France, James was only fifteen. She could feel life begin to change for the boys after that, for James in particular. In their Catholic village, the words Protestant and English had been words of hate. It was a great surprise to James when the Protestant English soldiers billeted in his home were likable, fun-loving human beings. In the evenings the soldiers would drill the older FitzGibbon boys in the kitchen, and laugh and play with the younger ones. Old prejudices fell away and horizons expanded for James.

One day when the corporal who had drilled their corps was suddenly ordered to join his regiment, the captain, newly returned from England and unfamiliar with the new system of drilling, attempted to put the men through their exercises. The ignorance and confusion of the corps drove the captain into a white-hot rage. While the older men stood speechless, young James stepped out and said, "The men are not to blame, sir. You are giving us words of command we have never heard." Then he stood there quaking, expecting the captain's wrath on his head.

Instead, after a pause of astonishment, the captain asked James to put the men through their exercises. The men did well and James was asked to go on drilling them. A few days later he found a sergeant's pike, sword, and sash sent to his house with an order appointing James FitzGibbon a sergeant over men much older than himself, his father and brother included.

Now the first lieutenant of the corps had been given a company in the new Tarbert Fencibles and had persuaded James to join as pay-sergeant. He was packed and ready to go to England. Would England satisfy him, his mother wondered? She prayed that the promise he had given her could hold him.

It held him for a little while. But in 1799, at age eighteen, James FitzGibbon left the Tarbert Fencibles and was drafted into the 49th Regiment as sergeant. He said afterward that he never intended to do it, but the persuasion of a recruiting general and the pressure of forty men who said they would volunteer only if FitzGibbon did had blotted out the promise to his mother.

When she read his letter, Mrs. FitzGibbon shuddered. There was little chance for a Catholic boy like James in the British army. Without money or friends in high places, his hope of obtaining a commission seemed nought. The odds were that he would remain a sergeant, subject to all the hardship, terrible danger, and possible degradation inherent in the army system. Still, James had a remarkable faculty for landing on his feet in whatever situation. Maybe ...

The morning after his enlistment he sailed for the invasion of Holland which landed him briefly in a French prison and erased all his misconceptions of the glories of war.

Two years later when he was twenty, he sailed under Lord Nelson against Denmark. Then in June of 1802, the 49th was sent to the Canadas to be stationed at Quebec. During the past three years, Fitz had served under Isaac Brock, a commander who was already his personal hero and who was destined to become the hero of Upper Canada. Brock, Lieutenant-Colonel of the 49th Regiment, combined all the best qualities of a British officer, qualities James and his mother had not dared hope to find in an army that was notorious for high-nosed arrogance, tyrannical discipline, and outright brutality. Isaac Brock tempered strict discipline with kindness, fairness, and faith in his men; and he gave them an example of personal courage, good humour, and pride. Under Brock, the 49th would earn the nickname of "Green Tigers," a title that aptly described their daring as well as the green facings on their jackets.

"Out of one of the worst regiments in the service," the Duke of York reported, "Colonel Brock has made the 49th one of the best." Out of the young impulsive boy from Ireland, Colonel Brock was making an outstanding soldier who would dare anything for his commander and for the British cause.

Brock had been quick to see the promise in young FitzGibbon. On the long voyage to Quebec he often smiled at the sight of James propped up in one of the swaying lifeboats surrounded by books of military tactics and field exercises. Isaac suspected that young FitzGibbon must have memorized the entire *Rules and Regulations for the Field Exercises of His Majesty's Forces* by the time they sighted land. On arrival at Quebec he promoted James to sergeant-major of the regiment over forty older sergeants.

The Canadas, Upper and Lower, were governed from London, with capitals at Quebec in Lower Canada and at York (Toronto) in Upper Canada. A governor-in-chief was stationed at Quebec and a lieutenant-governor at York. Although Europe was in a turmoil because of the Napoleonic wars, the Canadas, from 1802 to 1810, were mainly peaceful, without great adventure or opportunity for advancement. England had neither time nor troops to spare for a war in America, so those who governed and those who commanded in the Canadas were cautioned to keep a careful peace with neighbours to the south.

During these years, FitzGibbon was Brock's faithful sergeant-major; whenever the Colonel faced trouble, Fitz was there. In 1803 at York, when three soldiers took a military bateau and deserted across Lake Ontario, Brock took James and ten other men and set out at midnight to row across Lake Ontario and capture them.

Again in 1803, when mutiny broke out at Niagara's Fort George against the tyrannical authority of Colonel Sheaffe and news reached Isaac Brock at York, FitzGibbon was the man chosen to accompany him. Brock walked into the fort and, by sheer force of personality, made one of the ringleaders lay down his arms while the other one handcuffed him. He then had the drummer arouse the garrison and within a half hour had eleven mutineers handcuffed and on board the schooner for York. James FitzGibbon was then sent with the prisoners to Quebec where their trial took place.

During these years, Brock kept James supplied with books and taught him not only the arts of the military but the manners and lifestyle of a gentleman. He also taught him how to go about doing the impossible. Only once FitzGibbon had answered Brock that something was impossible. "By the Lord Harry, sir, do not tell me it is impossible," thundered Brock, "nothing should be impossible to a soldier. The word impossible should not be found in a soldier's dictionary."

FitzGibbon never forgot that. In 1807, when there was fear of American invasion, Brock ordered James to bring him twenty bateaux to embark troops for Montreal. FitzGibbon found the boats left high by the tide, separated by two hundred yards of mud from the water to float them. It would be impossible to move them. He had turned his men away when his imagination heard a familiar voice asking, "Did you try it, sir?"

"Front!" he ordered his men, "I think it impossible for us to put these bateaux afloat, but you know it will not do to tell the colonel so, unless we try it. Let us try — there are the boats. I am sure if it is possible for men to put them afloat, you will do it; go at them." In half an hour it was done.

Now, five years later, threatened invasion from the south was becoming fact. Naval blockades arising from Napoleon's Berlin Decree and Britain's answering Orders-in-Council had ended the peace. Britain's insistence that she search neutral ships for deserters and her habit of impressment of sailors who sometimes happened to be United States citizens infuriated many Americans. Although the northern states did not want war against the Canadas, the war party in Congress proved too strong for them. By the spring of 1812 you could taste war all along the frontier.

To James FitzGibbon it was a tangy exciting taste; it was the long-awaited opportunity for advancement. He applied to resign the adjutancy of the 49th Regiment in the hope that he might be given command of a company.

Sir George Prevost desires me
to inform you that he has this
instant received intelligence from
Mr. Richardson by an express
to the Northwest Company, an-
nouncing that the American
Government had declared war
against Great Britain.

Colonel Baynes to Major-General
Brock, Quebec, June 25, 1812.

2

The brigade of bateaux loaded with soldiers moved slowly into the St. Lawrence River from Lachine. Lieutenant James FitzGibbon filled his lungs with the clean river air. It was July of 1812. He was thirty-two years old and delighted to be moving up-country now that war with the United States was declared. Since his arrival in Quebec ten years before, he had travelled this river often and knew it in any mood. He had an uncanny instinct for geography and knew the shoreline from Quebec to Niagara with an accuracy that surprised even Indians and those fur-trader explorers called voyageurs who used rivers and lakes to push far inland and send rich furs home to England.

James FitzGibbon was well-satisfied just now; he had been given command of a company. He had a war, a command, a devotion to all things British, and a land he deemed worth fighting for. He might, of course, be killed fighting this war. But until then he would have action, excitement, possibly promotion — and he wanted above all things to get ahead in this world.

He had a heavy job getting fifteen boatloads of soldiers and

15

army provisions up this wild river. The bateaux were thirty to forty feet long and five to eight feet wide. The sides rose straight up to a height of four feet; the sharply pointed bow and stern came a foot higher. White oak formed the bottom, light fir the sides. These remarkably adaptable boats could be rowed, poled, and sailed, and they almost never capsized. Best of all they were flat-bottomed and could slide over the great boulders of the Cedars and Long Sault Rapids.

Now on Lac St. Louis, the French-Canadian boatmen had hoisted their lug sails, and the boats were sailing before a rare, light, east wind. Without a keel and a weather helm and with crude rigging, bateaux could only sail well before the wind which usually blew from the west.

Ahead lay the Cascades, the Cedars, and the Coteau Rapids. The attention of the entire brigade was fastened now on the scene before them as a bateau and a larger Durham boat come flying down the Cedars and Cascades. These rapids, because so shallow, were considered the most dangerous on the St. Lawrence. The two craft, caught up in the furious, churning, white madness, seemed to leap and plunge in the maelstrom. In one place, as FitzGibbon knew well, the long downhill plunge was like a mill race. But he and his soldiers heard the triumphant cries of *Vive Le Roi* as the boats rose out of that run, and his soldiers and boatmen answered with their own cheers of congratulation. It was a drama re-enacted daily, but not always happily, as burial crosses on the shoreline testified.

FitzGibbon's bateaux, bound upriver, had a few small locks to help them over the worst places. The first had been cut through limestone at Coteau du Lac in 1781. A few more had been crudely constructed to help the Loyalists move upriver, and in 1804 some of the locks had been improved and enlarged by the Royal Engineers. But for hour after hour, poling and tracking were the order of the hot July day. With the soldiers disembarked, the crew would thrust iron-tipped poles into the channel and work their way up the rocks, or the crewmen would jump into the water, often up to their armpits, and, with loops over their shoulders, haul or track the boats against the current while one oarsman left on board steered with a long sweep. When rough terrain made tracking impossible, boats had to be dragged over skidways made of logs.

The twenty-five miles of Lac St. Francis provided calm water again. At night, FitzGibbon's soldiers and crewmen bivouacked on the shore but they pressed on again by the early light of mid-summer dawn. From the Indian village of St. Regis at the foot of the nine-mile Long Sault Rapids, FitzGibbon kept his brigade against the south shore. This American shoreline was enemy territory where they might be ambushed at any time, but it also provided the easiest, swiftest route through the rapids, the one that his boatmen knew best. Time was important and risk was inevitable in time of war.

The river remains narrow and swift above the Long Sault, with small villages on either shore. By 1812 the south shore was more bustling and built-up than the north, but even on the Canadian shore the heavy forest was broken by a few well-kept farms like Crysler's above the Long Sault; the Loyalists' huts were being replaced by stout stone houses and small villages, like Matilda and Prescott. There was tension as they passed Prescott, for the St. Lawrence runs narrow here and raids were expected. Above Prescott they could lose themselves in the islands, and the soldiers could relax and laugh about what they'd do to 'em at Kingston or York or Fort Erie if they came a callin'.

FitzGibbon's nimble mind catalogued the countryside, the pretty town just passed on the left, established by Augusta Jones (later to be called Brockville), the pitch-pine trees on the island, the flight of wild ducks, herons, king-fishers, once a bald eagle. But another part of his mind staged battles, pondered methods of attack, ambush, surprise! Surprise was altogether important in small battles. He had a notion that war here in the Canadas would be a different sort of war than he had seen briefly in Europe. It might even be different from anything his senior officers expected or could handle.

Except Brock! Brock would know what he was about. Isaac Brock, the well-loved colonel of the 49th was now Major-General Isaac Brock, commander of the forces in Upper Canada. In the absence of Lieutenant-Governor Gore he was appointed Administrator of Upper Canada as well.

Grinning, Fitz recalled the time Brock had thundered at him, "By the Lord Harry, sir, do not tell me it is impossible." As he moved upriver now he was convinced that a full measure of the impossible lay ahead for the gallant major-general. This country was considered lost, not only in the opinion of aggressive Americans but in the opinion of most of the inhabitants. England had her hands full in Europe. While she dealt with Napoleon on the high seas and tried to stop his march by land, she could do little to defend what the French had dubbed a "few *arpents* of snow" in North America.

Altogether, Fitz knew there were only 4,450 regular soldiers in Upper and Lower Canada. The militia amounted to 2,500 men in Lower Canada, 1,800 in Upper Canada. Among the militia there were staunch Loyalists, veterans of the American Revolution who would fight like demons to keep this land British, but often they were old men; their sons were young and strong but they were also untried and untrained.

The task ahead for Brock, and officers like himself, was to occupy forts at Kingston, York (Toronto), Newark (Niagara), Chippawa, Fort Erie, Amherstburg, and St. Joseph. They had to escort convoys up the vulnerable St. Lawrence as Fitz was doing now. They had to defend 800 miles of frontier in Upper Canada alone. To the Americans, he knew they looked like a handful of redcoat-and-homespun which would surrender at the first volley. Henry Clay, speaker of the House of Representatives, looking northward with greedy eyes, had declared it "absurd to suppose we shall not succeed." Fitz had also heard that General Porter boasted he could take Upper Canada with a corporal and six men to carry a flag because the majority of its inhabitants were awaiting the chance to join the United States. His remark was not altogether foolish when one considered that British North America had only a half-million settlers against six million Americans, and that a large portion of the population of Upper Canada was of American origin.

As Fitz talked with the settlers along the shoreline, in Glengarry and Matilda and from Prescott to Kingston, he sensed the fear and uncertainty, sometimes even a willingness to be defeated, which enraged him. But occasionally he heard a new note of confidence now that they had a military administrator of the province. And the settlers in turn sensed something about this man FitzGibbon as he moved upriver with his robust soldiers. He was so utterly resolute, so eager. The farmer leaning on his hoe, the woman at her cottage door, felt a little better after he had passed.

Major-General Isaac Brock, as the new Administrator of Upper Canada, could combine the military and administrative authority of the country to move quickly when needed. If the impossible had to be done, at least they had the right man in the right place to do it. Fitz could go up the St. Lawrence to Kingston, full of confidence.

We are engaged in an awful and eventful contest. By unanimity and dispatch in our councils, and by vigour in our operation, we may teach the enemy this lesson – that a country defended by free men, enthusiastically devoted to the cause of their king and constitution, can never be conquered!

Major-General Brock to the Legislature at York, July 28, 1812.

3

As FitzGibbon moved upriver at the end of July, Major-General Isaac Brock in York was figuratively tearing out his hair. He had a war to fight and he could not get at it. At least he thought he had a war to fight, but he did not know that for sure, either.

As far back as February he had written to Governor Sir George Prevost, "Every day hostilities are retarded, the greater the difficulties we shall have to encounter." But war was not officially declared until June 18, and still, on July 28, as he opened a special session of the legislature, Brock did not know whether the Declaration of War had been passed by Congress.

Well aware that he was unequal to any American show of force (the population of the British colonies was half a million against six to eight million Americans), Brock considered his best weapon to be surprise. If he could move before his enemy was ready, he might deal a blow which would greatly inconvenience the Americans, which would delight the Indians and ally them to the British cause, and which would convince the faltering settlers that they could resist and ultimately win against the Americans.

His target was the American Fort Detroit. Detroit and Michilimackinac at the top of Lake Huron were fur trading posts which would control the western entrance to Upper Canada and must be in British hands before he had any hope of holding 800 miles of frontier with the 1,200 troops he had. On July 12, the American General Hull had arrived at Detroit and immediately crossed the St. Clair River to occupy the Canadian village of Sandwich (today's Windsor).

On July 28, Brock wrote to Governor Sir George Prevost in Quebec, "My situation is getting each day more critical. I still mean to try and send a force to the relief of Amherstburg [the British fort down the St. Clair River from Sandwich], but almost despair of succeeding."

At last on July 29, Isaac Brock received letters from the city of Quebec telling him war was officially declared. He now knew the name of the game he was playing. Then, from the west, came the good news that Captain Roberts, stationed at St. Joseph's Island where Lakes Huron and Michigan meet, had collected 180 voyageurs along with his forty-five regulars, borrowed boats from the North West Company and swept down to capture Fort Michilimackinac. Four hundred uncommitted Indians went along to watch. So surprised were the Americans that it never occurred to them to fight. Brock chuckled as he pictured their surrender and saw the British flag hoisted over the rocks and trees of that far wilderness.

Then, wonder of wonders, the men of York were stirring into action. He had just written of them earlier that day, "A full belief possesses them all that this Province must inevitably succumb. ... Most of the people have lost all confidence. ... I however speak loud and look big." Now here was the York militia volunteering their services to any part of the province. "I have selected 100 whom I have directed to proceed without delay to Long Point, where I propose collecting a force for the relief of Amherstburg," Brock wrote to Sir George Prevost on July 29.

As Brock made preparation to move toward Detroit, his mind also moved along the St. Lawrence and Niagara frontiers, reviewing the pitifully inadequate means of defence. In the months past, with great attention to detail, he had done what he could with the little he had. A system of convoy was established, with FitzGibbon bringing the first one up the St. Lawrence now, to move both regiments and war supplies up the St. Lawrence as soon as they could be spared from Quebec and Montreal. During spring, recruiting had gone on in Glengarry to form a new provincial corps known as the Glengarry Light Infantry; by May 14, Colonel Baynes, Adjutant-General, could report it complete to 400 rank and file. (Some of these men FitzGibbon would be destined to lead after his own 49th was worn to shreds by battle.)

An Inspecting Field Officer had moved through the line of settlements to check on the militia and set their quotas. Between Glengarry and Kingston, Brock had urged every man capable of bearing a musket to be prepared to act, and he had noted the need for a rallying point and stronghold in the vicinity of Prescott. As FitzGibbon's first convoy passed Prescott in July, his soldiers waved at carpenters at work on a new fortification to be known as Fort Wellington. Farmers with heavy teams were drawing timbers and stones for the construction. It cheered the soldiers to know there would be protection in the future for this vulnerable, narrow stretch of the St. Lawrence.

Meanwhile, at York and Niagara, Brock had called out flank companies of militia which would be drilled much like regular soldiers and used in heavy fighting. This produced a force of 800 men, all in need of blankets, haversacks, kettles, and tents. From Fort George he wrote, "The militia assembled in a wretched state in regard to clothing; many were without shoes, an article which can scarcely be provided in the country." These 800 untested soldiers without shoes would have the task of defending the Niagara River line until British soldiers could be moved up from Quebec and Kingston. And that depended on regiments being spared from the colossal fight in which Britain was engaged against Napoleon in Europe.

Then there was the question of food. Back in February he wrote that he had directed the Assistant Deputy Commissary-General at Amherstburg to purchase 2,000 bushels of Indian corn. "Corn will be absolutely necessary in the event of war." Shrewdly he added, "It is to be procured, if possible, on the American side, that our own stock may remain undiminished."

An American spy, writing to his superiors, expressed envious admiration at Brock's preparations. "General Brock has paid attention to every particular that can relate to the future resources of the Province. The harvest has been got in tolerably well and greater preparation is making for sowing grain than was ever made before. The militia duty is modified as much as possible to suit the circumstances of the people and measures taken to prevent them from feeling the burden of the war. The women work in the field, encouragement being given for the purpose."

But Brock, as he embarked for Amherstburg, knew it was not enough. Only a bold stroke could weld British soldier, settler, and Indian into a fighting force that would not blow to pieces in the first wind from the south. On August 6 he left York with the York Volunteers for Burlington Bay where they travelled overland to Long Point on Lake Erie. Here he picked up the Norfolk militia under George Ryerson and embarked 260 militia and forty soldiers of the 41st Regiment in a collection of leaky boats. At Port Talbot, they were joined by Peter Robinson and his riflemen.

If James FitzGibbon knew of Brock's trek to Detroit, he must have longed to be with him. He would have thoroughly enjoyed this 200-mile trip along the Lake Erie shore, with excitement guaranteed at the end of it. But James must either have been in Kingston or moving down the St. Lawrence in order to bring up another convoy. Instead it was the young men of York County, untried militia, who swept this unique flotilla along at the rapid pace Brock set from his bateaux headquarters. Stormy weather beat upon the men and drenched them as they battled rough water under the red clay cliffs on the north shore. In the night there was no rest for men weary at the oars; the light they followed at the bow of Brock's own bateau kept bobbing rapidly over the water, pressing westward.

As Brock moved through the Lake Erie night, his mind played on some American documents he had had the good luck to read. General William Hull and his weary, nervous American army of 2,500 men had marched through swampy country to the shores of Lake Erie where he had hired the schooner *Cayahoga* to take their heavy baggage, medical stores, and musical instruments to

Fort Detroit. But the *Cayahoga* had been captured by the British brig, *General Hunter*, and Hull's official correspondence to the Secretary of War found on board. It was swiftly carried to Brock at Fort George, and it had shown in Hull a despondency and want of initiative, which cheered Brock's heart.

Now as he arrived at Amherstburg just before midnight on the night of August 13, he found more pleasant reading, this time brought in by Tecumseh, the Shawanese chief. With twenty-five warriors, Tecumseh had ambushed a party of 200 Americans sent out from Detroit to escort supplies; he had captured the provisions bound for Hull as well as another batch of Hull's letters, still full of doubt and fear.

The meeting of Brock and Tecumseh, as it comes to us through the pen and paintbrush of those who watched, is one of the most dramatic moments in Canadian history. Each had heard of the other. The general stood, tall and broad-shouldered in his scarlet tunic and white pants, his eyes blue and steady in a strong but amiable face framed by fair hair; the Shawanese chief was smaller, but supple and perfectly built. His copper face was oval, his hair shining black over dark piercing eyes that took the measure of Brock. Born within a year of one another, and with backgrounds worlds apart, fate was joining their destinies and they both seemed to know it. They would die within a year of each other, too. From this moment of their meeting a unique rapport was evident between them. Tecumseh smiled and said to one of his Indians in his own tongue, "This is a man!" On a later occasion his perceptive admiration of Brock's character was expressed in terse, simple words, "Other chiefs say, 'Go' – General Brock says, 'Come.'"

Brock put his feelings for Tecumseh in a letter the following day to Lord Liverpool, British Secretary of State for War. "He who most attracted my attention was a Shawnee Chief, Tecumseh, the brother of The Prophet, who for the last two years had carried on, contrary to our remonstrances, an active war against the United States. A more sagacious or a more gallant warrior does not, I believe, exist. He was the admiration of everyone who conversed with him."

It was Tecumseh who supplied Brock with details of the ter-

24

rain around Fort Detroit. (Hull had withdrawn from Sandwich across the river into his fort on August 7.) On a roll of bark Tecumseh's scalping-knife drew the river, then the hills, the clearings, the muskeg and forest and network of trails that would serve Brock's little army. But that night in private council, Brock was unable to convince Colonel Henry Procter and his other officers to attack. Procter had 250 regulars at Amherstburg and 150 militia. Altogether they would have 300 regulars and 400 militia. Suddenly he stopped the useless arguing and announced that he had made a decision. They would cross the river and attack Fort Detroit.

At dawn the Indians were told of his decision. Tecumseh remarked that their great father, King George, had awakened out of a long sleep. Tecumseh's hatred of the Americans knew no bounds and the men of the 4th U.S. Regiment, now holding Fort Detroit, were his special enemies. Less than a year before, under General Harrison, they had slaughtered his half-armed band of 600 men and women on the banks of the Tippecanoe River while he and his warriors were away.

In the afternoon, Brock moved to Sandwich opposite Fort Detroit and occupied the mansion of Colonel Baby. Macdonell and Glegg, his two aides-de-camp, were sent off to Hull with a dispatch demanding his immediate surrender. "It is far from my intention to join in a war of extermination," Brock had written, "but you must be aware that the numerous body of Indians who have attached themselves to my troops will be beyond control the moment the contest commences." In actual fact Brock had a promise from Tecumseh that the scalping knife would not be used tomorrow; and Tecumseh was rare among North American chiefs in that he did not use torture.

The trails north of Sandwich, visible from Fort Detroit, were alive with marching men. They were the same men, marching back and forth, crossing and recrossing – Brock's few soldiers and Tecumseh's braves attempting to make their army look double its actual size. Major Thomas Evans had craftily clothed the western militia in cast-off uniforms of the 41st Regiment which gave them twice the number of regulars in the eyes of the Americans.

For the past week, soldiers had worked in the dark of night to set up a battery in a grove of oak trees opposite Fort Detroit. By the time Brock received Hull's answer that he would not surrender, the battery was ready. In the night, on August 15, the trees were cut down. In the morning Brock's force of 330 regulars and 400 militia, with 600 Indians under Tecumseh, crossed the Detroit River. Slowly the columns were formed, and the steady tramp of determined men sounded on the trails to Fort Detroit. Two 24-pounders which Hull had placed in their path, and the long heavy guns of Fort Detroit, looked them in the eyes and waited.

Meanwhile, the batteries, revealed to the Americans by the morning light, opened fire. The first shot fired in the War of 1812 crashed into the American fort and killed an American officer who was a close friend of the British artillerymen who trained the gun. Now Hull's 24-pounders answered the British guns and shells, and round shot flew in both directions across the river. But an 18-pound shell from one of the British guns crashed through an embrasure in the officers' mess and killed four men. Hull made up his mind. The British troops, expecting grapeshot and hellfire at any second as they advanced, saw instead a white flag of truce. Simultaneously, another white flag was crossing the river to silence the Sandwich battery. It was over. Hull was surrendering his army of 2,500 to 330 British, 400 militia, and 600 Indians.

4

Every three or four miles, on
every eminence, Brock has erec-
ted a snug battery, the last saucy
argument of kings, poking their
white noses and round black nos-
trils right upon your face, ready
to spit fire and brimstone in your
very teeth, if you were to offer to
turn squatter on John Bull's land.

John Lovett (General Van Rensselaer's military secretary) to a
friend, Lewiston, 1812.

As the news swept east from Detroit, a wave of dis-
belief, then joy, swept the Canadas. Captain Glegg took despatches and the colours of the 4th U.S. Regiment to Sir
George Prevost in the city of Quebec. After he had passed, people in the streets of York walked taller. There was rowdy laughter in the barrack rooms at Niagara and Kingston. FitzGibbon
and his friends talked with admiration of this man Tecumseh. A
flotilla of provisions moving up the St. Lawrence stopped mo-
mentarily as French-Canadian oarsmen and British soldiers gave
a lusty cheer. Lieutenant George Ryerson bearing the news to
the Talbot settlement stopped the night in an Indian camp
where aged warriors and women chanted songs of victory all
night. From Fort George, an urgent message was sent to Kingston asking for three companies of the 49th Regiment and a detachment of the Newfoundland Regiment. The hourly expected
arrival of the prisoners from Detroit might place Fort George in
the awkward position of having more prisoners than soldiers.

Fort George, situated on the west bank of the Niagara River
about one mile from Lake Ontario and opposite the American

Fort Niagara, consisted of six small bastions connected by picket fencing twelve feet in height with room for 220 men and a spacious officers' quarters. The town of Newark, later Niagara, nestled against its rather dubious protection. Vessels of over fifty tons could sail past Newark up the Niagara River as far as Queenston, where the portage around Niagara Falls began. Even without war this portage road was a bustling street with sometimes fifty farm wagons at work on it. Salt pork and flour and trading goods moved up the river while North West Company furs and wheat, corn, oats, and fruit from the farms around Niagara and farther west, moved down.

But on August 25, 1812, a parade of victory came down the Queenston road as the Detroit expedition returned. We can best see it in perspective by crossing over to the American side where no one described it better than John Lovett, secretary to General Van Rensselaer. Lovett always turned the clear light of humour on those pompous British across the river but he shone an equally brilliant searchlight on the humiliation of his fellow Americans.

> It [yesterday] was a day of turmoil, mortification and humiliation through our camp. Such a flood as the consequences of Gen. Hull's surrender poured in upon us that it required considerable nerve to meet everything. ... Yesterday the first we saw was a guard of about 50 men passing with some wagons on the opposite shore; it was the victorious Brock returning to Fort George. He sent over Col. McDonald, his aide-de-camp, and Major Evans, two strapping lads in scarlet, gold and arms, to make a communication to General Van Rensselaer.
>
> I was ever proud of my country, and as an American could look any man of any nation at least *horizontally* in the face. But yesterday my eyes seemed to have acquired a new attachment to the ground.

In another letter, he wrote, "Before and behind, on the right and on the left, their proud victors gleamed in arms and their heads erect in the pride of victory. ... I think the line, including wagons, pleasure carriages, etc., was half a mile long, scattered.

The sensations this scene produced in our camp were inexpressible; mortification, indignation, fearful apprehension, suspicion, jealousy, dismay, rage, madness."

Many Americans had planned to draw the closing curtains swiftly on this Canadian play. One Massachusetts general officer had offered to "capture Canada by contract, raise a company of soldiers and take it in six weeks." Or, as Dearborn had written to Van Rensselaer, "At all events we must calculate on possessing Canada before the winter sets in." Now these men were stunned.

Aboard the schooner *Chippewa*, sailing down Lake Erie, Isaac Brock had just suffered a rude shock himself. The schooner *Lady Prevost* had hailed his ship and brought news of an armistice. Brock, with plans already in his head for the taking of Fort Niagara, exploded in anger. An armistice was a stupid blunder. It would give the Americans time to transport stores and men to the Niagara frontier where the next fight would take place; it would give them time to build naval power on the lakes. Right now Brock believed (and most historians still agree with him) that he could have taken Fort Niagara. Prevost, however, still believed peace was possible. The irritating, British Orders-in-Council had been repealed and he believed that meant that war could be avoided. But Prevost failed to understand the Americans. He underestimated their expansionist belief in "manifest destiny," their conviction that Canada could and should be theirs.

On September 4, Kingston greeted the arrival of Brock with spontaneous celebration. FitzGibbon is a hard man to keep track of in these busy days; it is possible he was there and talked with Brock and that this would be the last time they met. Or he may have been at Montreal or on the river again. Twelve days later, on September 16, he was bringing a convoy upriver when he was attacked near Prescott. Americans, with a gunboat and a Durham boat, left Ogdensburg opposite Prescott in the dark and landed at Toussaint Island near the spot where FitzGibbon's bateaux lay for the night. While the Americans seized the only family that lived on the island, one man escaped their notice. British to the core, the man plunged into the St. Lawrence and swam for the Canadian shore. He reached it, warned Fitz-Gibbon, and rallied the local militia. When the Americans attacked, soldiers and militia were ready for them. In the fray the Yankees had to abandon their Durham boat which drifted into Canadian hands. When the American gunboat and brigade exchanged fire, five of the eighteen on the gunboat were wounded. But the others on board turned a cannon on the British, and Fitz-Gibbon had to move his boats out of range. The Americans by this time had had enough and scurried back to Ogdensburg with their wounded. FitzGibbon's party, somewhat elated by this first encounter with the enemy, pressed on to Kingston.

On September 18, from Niagara, Brock wrote of his old regiment. "Six companies of the 49th are with me here, and the remaining four at Kingston, under Vincent. Although the regiment has been ten years in this country, drinking rum without bounds, it is still respectable and apparently ardent for an opportunity to acquire distinction." The burning of Fort George later in the war destroyed the papers of the 49th which could have showed whether FitzGibbon was with the six companies at Niagara or the four in Kingston, or still engaged in convoy duty, so we must go through the Battle of Queenston Heights not knowing for certain whether he took part. Since he never, in his writings, mentions the battle, it seems likely that he was in Kingston or on the St. Lawrence, chaffing to be there.

On September 8, President Madison ended the armistice. Tension tightened along the thirty-six miles of frontier from Fort George to Fort Erie. Brock kept his officers galloping along the river road to the guns at Brown's Point and Voorman's Point, to Queenston and Chippawa and Fort Erie, in a frenzy of organizing, despatching, informing and reviewing, tightening and strengthening, in whatever way he could, their thin red line of defence.

On October 9, at Fort Erie where the Niagara River flows out of Lake Erie, an enterprising young American named Lieutenant Elliot attacked and boarded the brigs *Detroit* and *Caledonia*. The *Detroit* was an American ship taken from General Hull at Detroit, the *Caledonia*, a brig of the North West Fur Company. Elliot's party managed to get the *Caledonia* over to the American batteries at Black Rock. The *Detroit* they burned when the firing from the Fort Erie garrison became too hot. Elliot gave the Americans their first shot of confidence since Hull's disaster.

On the night of October 11, a tremendous northeast storm brought thunder, lightning, and rain in torrents. Rain was still coming down as Brock and his staff sat late in council on the night of the twelfth. Then, at 4:15 in the morning of the thirteenth, Brock was awakened by cannon fire and recognized the noise of the big gun at Voorman's Point. Within moments he was on his horse Alfred and away, orders left behind to "Inform Colonel Macdonell and Major Glegg that I am off for Queenston. They are to follow, with all speed."

The seven-mile ride, along the river road from Fort George to Queenston, was Brock's last. His cloak streamed behind him as his horse pounded through the pre-dawn gloom. The dawn when it came would be spectacular, lighting up the mist over the blue Niagara and sending horizontal light through the coloured trees, iridescent and alive with rain and wind.

Brock's ears were tuned to the guns. Their different notes put together in his mind a sound picture of what was happening, the 24-pounder at Voorman's Point answering the guns of Lewiston across the river, the more distant punctuation of the 3-pounders and the brass 6-pounders at Queenston, and the roar of the 18-pounder that was halfway up Queenston Heights in a V-shaped redan battery. At Brown's Point, two miles below Queenston, he found the company of York Volunteers on the move toward Queenston, and waved them on. He galloped past the big gun at Voorman's. From Samuel Peter Jarvis of the York Volunteers, who galloped past him on a horse bound for Fort George, he had heard, "The Americans are crossing the river in force, sir."

Lights were burning in all the houses, and women and children huddled together. The bells of the church and courthouse at Niagara were ringing. In pursuit of Brock, his two aides, Macdonell and Glegg, spurred their horses along the river road.

Queenston is seven miles upriver from Fort George and here Brock reached the Niagara Escarpment where the land rises vertically 300 feet above the village of Queenston. Niagara Falls tumbled over here 12,000 years ago before it wore itself back seven miles to its present site, forming, as it retreated, the Niagara Gorge.

Brock galloped through the village and halfway up Queenston Heights for a view of what was happening on the river below. It was daylight now. More than a thousand Americans, led by Colonel Solomon Van Rensselaer, a cousin to the General, had landed and sought shelter under the brow of the Heights, awaiting reinforcements. The 49th grenadiers under Dennis and the York militia with a 3-pounder were near the river firing on the invaders. High on the Heights, Captain Williams had the 49th light infantry behind the 18-pounder which poured down destruction on the boats trying to cross the river. Then Brock ordered Williams' company down the hill to help Dennis. Down at the river a young American, Captain Wool, took command when Stephen Van Rensselaer was put out of action with multiple wounds. Captain Wool saw the British movement down the hill and, in a bold stroke, took his men up a fisherman's path, supposedly unassailable, to arrive thirty yards above the redan battery. When he saw American blue above him, Brock had no choice. He spiked the gun and his twelve men at the battery fled down the hill leaving the Americans in command of Queenston Heights.

With Williams' company behind him, Brock attempted to take back the Heights. George Jarvis was there, and told what happened:

> On arriving at the foot of the mountain, where the road diverges to St. David's, General Brock dismounted, and waving his sword, climbed over a high stone wall, followed by his troops. Placing himself at the head of the light company of the 49th, he led the way up the mountain at double-quick time, in the very teeth of a sharp fire from the enemy's rifle-men, and ere long he was singled out by one of them, who, coming forward, took deliberate aim, and fired. Several of the men noticed the action and fired, but too late, and our gallant General fell on his left side, within a few feet of where I stood. Running up to him, I enquired, "Are you much hurt sir?" He placed his hand on his breast, but made no reply, and sank down.

Two flank companies of militia (the York Volunteers) were under Lieutenant-Colonel John Macdonell, Brock's aide-de-camp, at Brown's Point. Macdonell, only twenty-five years of age, was Attorney-General of Upper Canada. When the news reached him, he rushed his 190 men to the Heights and tried to avenge Brock. The Americans had reinforcements now, 500 men on the Heights. The terrible rage of Macdonell and his men forced Captain Wool back up the hill and made him spike the 18-pounder gun. But suddenly both Macdonell and Williams fell seriously wounded. Macdonell's wounds were fatal although he lived for twenty-four hours in great agony.

Their leaders gone, the men were in disorder. It was ten A.M.; the day was already disastrous for the British and Canadians. The shattered soldiers fell back to Voorman's Point to wait for reinforcements, while the Americans conveyed wounded across the river and brought over fresh troops. The death of Brock had stunned every man. His body lay nearby in Durham's farm-house. Macdonell lay there, too, dying. The dreadful news swept along the frontier.

At Fort Erie, Captain Driscoll of the 100th Regiment tells how a dragoon galloped up and gave the news to an "old green tiger" who seemed unable to tell it to his comrades. "I placed my hand on his shoulder, 'For heaven's sake, tell us what you know.' In choking accents he revealed his melancholy information. 'General Brock is killed, the enemy has possession of Queenston Heights.' Every man in the battery was paralyzed. They ceased firing. A cheer from the enemy on the opposite side of the river recalled us to our duty. They had heard of their success down the river."

In the other direction, the news reached Fort George where British guns were attempting to silence the guns of Fort Niagara across the river. In command at Fort George, was Major-General Roger Hale Sheaffe, whose orders from Brock were to follow as soon as he could ascertain where the enemy meant to make their real attack.

Sheaffe reached Voorman's at about eleven o'clock, then took a back route through St. David's to come upon the Heights two miles west of the Americans with a collected force of 800 men.

Lieutenant John Norton (a Scotsman married to an Indian girl), with one hundred Indians, led Sheaffe on a route that took the Americans completely by surprise. Forced to face Sheaffe's long advancing line, the Americans found their backs to the river wall, their lives balanced on a precipice above the Niagara gorge. Sheaffe was in front of them, Queenston forces on the right and Indians were terrifying their left. Wool was wounded and succeeded by Colonel Winfield Scott, who tried to keep his men in order.

Meanwhile across the river at Lewiston, General Van Rensselaer was attempting to get reinforcements to his men on Queenston Heights. His secretary, Lovett, once more tells us how it was over there: "Still the reinforcements moved over very slowly and, in short, stopped. The General returned to accelerate them. He mounted a borrowed horse and I rode with him, everywhere urging on the troops, for not half of them had passed over. But the name of Indian, or the sight of the wounded, or the devil or *something else* petrified them. Not a regiment, not a company, scarcely a man would go."

Now the Americans on the Heights were in complete panic. They fled down the cliff and attempted to swim the Niagara. Many threw themselves off the Heights. At three o'clock Colonel Winfield Scott raised the white flag and surrendered 300 soldiers and officers to the British. Six hundred more would be routed out of hiding the following day.

The bright joy of victory was darkened by the overwhelming grief at the death of Brock. For less than two months these colonies had had a hero larger than life. Now they had a dead hero.

In the dark hours of the night, Brock's surviving aide-de-camp sat alone writing it down on paper. In a letter to Mr. William Brock, he wrote:

> With a heart agonized with most painful sorrow, I am compelled by duty and affection to announce to you the death of my most valuable and ever to be lamented friend, your brother, Major-General Brock. ... His loss at any time would have been great to his relations and friends, but at this moment I consider the melancholy event as a public calamity. He was beloved and esteemed by all who had the

happiness to know him, and was adored by his army and by the inhabitants of the Province.

General Brock and Macdonell were buried on October 17 in the northeast battery at Fort George. The coffins were preceded first by a company of regulars, then a band of music, and followed by another body of regulars and militia. The distance between Government House and the garrison was lined by a double row of militia men and Indians, resting on their arms reversed. Minute guns were fired during the whole procession. Across the river the American guns of Lewiston and Fort Niagara fired minute-guns, "as a mark of respect to a brave enemy."

Van Rensselaer had been opposed to this war in the first place; within days he would resign and hand over the Niagara command to General Smythe.

Major-General Sheaffe, Brock's successor, had agreed to another armistice without any apparent reason. It was not approved by Sir George Prevost who seemed to understand Brock's position once Brock was dead. The armistice applied only to the Niagara frontier between Lakes Erie and Ontario and could be terminated on twenty-four hours notice. It was to last until the Americans ended it on November 20.

For the month after Brock's death Upper Canada could talk of nothing else. There were a few then, and historians later, who ventured to suggest that Brock was rash, that he should have protected his own life and lived to fight another day. But the questions remain: without the gallant example of that scarlet figure out in front, would the Canadas have struggled to their feet at all? Without a hero who could size up the desperate odds and attempt desperate measures, had they any chance against the American giant?

If anyone understood Brock's fighting philosophy, it was the men of the 49th Regiment. Trained in the tactics of speed and surprise, they were quick with admiration for honesty, fairness, and personal bravery. The "old green tiger" at Fort Erie who was stunned to silence by the news of Brock's death had quickly recovered himself and he and his comrades "now exhibited demoniac energy" as their guns gave it to Black Rock "hot and heavy."

This demoniac energy was to characterize the 49th Regiment in the two hard years of fighting ahead. Brock somehow was their leader in death as he was in life. His scarlet figure beckoning up the heights of Queenston seemed to stand before them whether at Niagara or Stoney Creek or Crysler's Farm on the St. Lawrence.

And from Detroit the words of Tecumseh rang out, "Other chiefs say, 'Go' – General Brock says, 'Come.'"

5

FitzGibbon was a fine man, and a splendid soldier. The men adored him, although he was strict. His word was law, and they had such faith in him that I believe if he had told any one of them to jump into the river, he would have obeyed. He always knew what he was about, and his men knew it, and had full confidence in him.

M. Le Lievre, of Three Rivers, speaking in 1873 of convoy expeditions in 1812.

It is 450 miles by road from Montreal to Niagara, slightly less by water. Almost 600 miles separate Amherstburg from Montreal. This was a long lifeline and if the Americans severed it at any point, everything to the west of that severence was lost.

The battles might wait for spring but the lifeline of supply throbbed with activity in the cold of the Canadian winter as troops and guns and provisions made their way up-country. In January, 1813, James FitzGibbon was in charge of forty-five sleighs loaded with military stores, making the 250-mile trip from Kingston to Niagara in the coldest temperatures of the year. This was probably his first movement to the Niagara frontier since war broke out, and his eagerness to get there must have kept him warm. The news of Brock's death would have hit him as hard as any man; Brock had been an older brother to him, a teacher, a hero, and a friend. At least he was moving to the site where Brock had died and to the most likely place for the next attack. At Niagara he could do something to help what Isaac Brock had died for.

For a while he could keep his brigade within the shelter of what is today Prince Edward County, travelling the snow and ice of the Bay of Quinte. But once he crossed the narrow bridge of land known as Carrying Place, he left all protection behind and faced the buffeting force of the January winds that swept Lake Ontario. Still it was better here than travelling the snow-filled roads through the forests on shore. Doggedly now they kept on. The enthusiasm of FitzGibbon was contagious, and his men felt the challenge even as they felt the cold. The grim-visaged beauty of this land was not lost on FitzGibbon. After ten years in this country he knew winter in its every mood and its hard white beauty excited him. His affinity for the landscape and his quick commitment to memory of shorelines, contours, rivers, pathways, and roads would be an important asset in the role he would play in this war. Even now, in a white cauldron of wind on an open lake, FitzGibbon always knew where he was.

They reached Niagara, and he was sent with his company to the west shore of Lake Erie to guard Detroit against an American attack across the frozen lake. There had been trouble here on January 22, when the American Army of the West, under Generals Harrison and Winchester, attacked twenty-five miles south of Detroit on the River Raisin in an attempt to take back Michigan. With his Indian allies under Tecumseh, Colonel Procter had defeated them and taken 600 prisoners. Here, Fitz probably met Tecumseh, and it may have been from his warriors that he learned to admire and imitate Indian skills in forest warfare.

In April, FitzGibbon and his men came back to Frenchman's Creek on the Niagara River, four miles from Fort Erie. Winter here had been quiet but there was news of a successful attack from Prescott on Ogdensburg, across the river, intended to stop the American raiding parties which had continued ever since the attack on FitzGibbon's convoy last fall. The Canadian attackers were led by Lieutenant-Colonel "Red" George Macdonell, a relative of John Macdonell, Brock's aide-de-camp, slain at Queenston. His Glengarry Light Infantry Fencibles fought with the tenacity which would distinguish them throughout the war.

The ice breaking up on the Niagara River had an ominous

sound in the spring of 1813; the armies on both sides of the river knew what lay ahead. FitzGibbon was too restless to wait for the larger action of the war. On April 6, he was scouting the river when the rays of the setting sun revealed movement on the American shore, and he saw a dug-out boat move toward Strawberry Island. He and a sergeant jumped in a boat, paddled over, and "pounced on them as nose to nose, one was giving to his friend the light from his cigar." Then his sharp eyes saw a second dug-out leave the American shore. He hid himself close to the landing to take them prisoners as well.

But larger action was imminent, in fact, already afloat. It was obvious to both sides that whoever controlled the water supply routes could win this war. General Dearborn had command of the American Army's Military District No. 9, from Lake Erie to Vermont. Based at Sackett's Harbour at the east end of Lake Ontario was Commodore Isaac Chauncey, rapidly building a sizable fleet to control Lake Ontario.

The British were obviously in for trouble on the water. Their ships were the *Royal George*, the *Earl of Moira*, the *Sir Sidney Smith*, the *Duke of Gloucester* and the *Prince Regent*, as well as the *Wolfe* just coming off the stocks at Kingston. Another new ship, the *Sir Isaac Brock* was being built at York. But in the race for power the Americans were pulling ahead. Moreover, the British lacked officers. Sir James Yeo, who would dance a nautical ballet with Chauncey through 1813 and 1814, was on his way to the Canadas but he would not arrive in Kingston until May 15.

On April 27, at seven in the morning, the American fleet under Chauncey attacked York. General Sheaffe himself was there but his soldiers were at Fort George and along the Niagara frontier. At York he had 300 regular troops, 200 militia and 100 Indians, as the Americans began to land 1,700 troops west of old Fort Rouillé. Another thousand seamen remained on board the fourteen vessels which had trained one hundred guns on Fort York. Sheaffe's 700 regulars marched out of Fort York to meet on the lakeshore but soon fell back to their first battery, then their second. It was no use. They spiked the guns of the second battery and retreated into the fort.

At the second battery, the American General Pike paused while he sent a party ahead to discover if the British had cleared out. As Pike suspected, they were gone, making rapid footsteps toward Kingston. Only the militia remained. Suddenly a dreadful explosion turned the world upside down as a powder magazine exploded. The true cause of the explosion has never been discovered but 100 Canadians and 250 Americans were killed or wounded. General Pike was one of them.

On the death of General Pike, General Dearborn landed. By 4 P.M. the American flag flew over York. Angered at the dreadful carnage of the explosion, American soldiers burned and pillaged the helpless town. Before his retreat, Sheaffe had ordered the new ship on the stocks to be burned. Fortunately, the *Prince Regent* was gone to Kingston. There remained one ship, *The Duke of Gloucester*, to be captured by the Americans.

Sheaffe would be severely criticized for his retreat although he had little choice, outnumbered three to one, his fort without large guns. But could he have prepared better for the defence of York? There were guns at York for the new ship being built which, if mounted on the fort, might have held off Chauncey's ships.

Although he had won the Battle of Queenston Heights and received a baronetcy from the British Parliament, Sheaffe would never become a hero in the Canadas. Too many soldiers, like Fitz-Gibbon, remembered the harsh treatment of his men that had led to mutiny at Fort George in 1803. There were also many who resented the armistice he signed after Queenston Heights when he could have swept across the river and taken Fort Niagara. On May 26, Sir George Prevost wrote to Lord Bathurst that he wanted to remove Sheaffe from Upper Canada: "It is my intention to place the civil administration and military command of Upper Canada in the hands of Major-General De Rottenburg, and Major-General Sir R. Sheaffe will return to Lower Canada."

FitzGibbon's granddaughter in her book, *A Veteran of 1812*, suggests that James was at York when it was captured. She says that he was frequently employed in conveying dispatches from the frontier to headquarters at Kingston. He seems a likely man for such errands for few soldiers could move faster or more surely over the face of the land. He may have been sent there after the attack for a first-hand report on the calamity.

He was soon back at Fort George to face what was coming next. Everyone knew the American attack on York was a preliminary; Dearborn and Chauncey would waste little time before striking Fort George. In command of Lake Ontario, those two were riding a wave of confidence now.

Chauncey sailed over to Fort Niagara to deposit Dearborn and his land force there on May 8, then sailed away to Sackett's Harbour with his wounded and his plunder from York. By May 25, he was back at Niagara, his guns firing on Fort George. Although Vincent had five 24-pounders from Fort Detroit, he was so short of powder that he could not answer Chauncey's guns. Reports came in to Fort George that Dearborn now had 6,000 land troops in Fort Niagara, poised for the moment of attack.

General John Vincent at Fort George had 1,400 regular soldiers and little faith in the militiamen of the province. "With respect to the militia, it is with regret that I can neither report favorably of their numbers nor their willing co-operation." He described them as "wavering and appalled by the specious force of the enemy's resources."

Vincent was slow to understand these men. They were farmers, and this was May, spring-planting time. Before the year was done, the British army would be glad of every grain of wheat they had tenaciously put in the ground that anxious spring. But if he thought they would stand by and give up their crops and their homes to Americans when the moment of decision came, he was wrong. Right now soldier and settler alike were facing terrible odds, and they had no daring Isaac Brock to cheer them toward the impossible. Their leader lay dead in the northeast bastion of Fort George and that knowledge still lay heavy on their hearts. Nor would they find another of his like throughout the war. Leaders would come and go on the Niagara frontier in 1813 and 1814, but often the inspiration would come from below, from junior officers like James FitzGibbon, militiamen like William Hamilton Merritt, and women like Laura Secord.

Vincent's 1,400 men were divided into three divisions. Fitz-

Gibbon was under Lieutenant-Colonel Harvey who had command of the right, from Fort George to Brown's Point. Vincent himself was at the centre in command of the fort. On the left along Lake Ontario to Four Mile Creek, was Colonel Myers. Early on the morning of May 27 a thick fog on the lake shrouded the American ships as they landed 6,000 troops under Colonel Winfield Scott.

Within three hours the contest was decided. The British left wing under Colonel Myers had suffered severely from the onslaught of troops landing and from the fire from the ships. Fort George and the entire peninsula-plateau was caught in a crossfire from the lake and the mouth of the river; the log buildings of the fort were on fire. At twelve o'clock, Major Glegg wrote a hasty note to Colonel William Claus in charge of Fort George. "The General desires you will immediately evacuate the Fort and join him on the Queenston road." The guns of Fort George were spiked, the ammunition destroyed, and the troops put in motion to march eighteen miles across country to the house of John DeCew near the Beaver Dams.

Earlier Vincent had written to Sir George Prevost about the DeCew house. "I have considered it expedient to establish a depot of ammunition and provisions, in a very central and commanding position near a place called the Beaver Dams, in a stone house belonging to a captain of militia who is a loyal and faithful subject."

John DeCew had built his spacious limestone house just before the war, high on the Niagara Escarpment overlooking deep valleys and varied hills. At DeCew Falls he set up saw and grist mills. Early in the war he offered his house as a supply depot for the army.

The weary soldiers retreated in remarkably good order, the rear guard holding off the Americans now taking possession of the Niagara frontier. In the houses of Newark and Queenston, women and children clung together facing the terrible decision to abandon their homes or stay within enemy lines. The rear guard reached DeCew's house sometime during the night and were soon joined by Lieutenant-Colonel Bisshopp with all the troops from Chippawa to Fort Erie.

In the morning Vincent found "all the militia of the country" flocking to him at DeCew's. If the British army was ready to retreat, the militia was not. William Hamilton Merritt, born at the mouth of the Twelve Mile Creek* where St. Catharines is today, was nineteen years old when war broke out and, as a militia dragoon, committed himself to the cause. He and the rest of the militia expected

> we would give them battle and prevent their penetrating in the country. However, to our great surprise and annoyance, an order was issued for all the waggons to be impressed and the army to retreat to the Forty. As many of the militia as chose to follow might, the rest were at liberty to return to their respective families. I strongly suspected from the indifferent manner the militia were treated the upper part of the Province was to be abandoned, as did all the militia, consequently numbers went home. ...
>
> In the evening I followed, overtook the General at the Forty Mile Creek, where I learnt we were to retreat to Burlington. The militia was given no encouragement to follow the army whatever; very few but what went back from this, as they were confident the army would not stop till we arrived at Kingston.

At least one British soldier agreed with the militiamen who wanted to fight. FitzGibbon could not believe they were giving up the Niagara Peninsula. But Vincent, pushed by an advancing American army, was moving all the way back to Burlington.

He had a strong position there on the height of land at the end of Burlington Bay where Dundurn Castle stands today, in the city of Hamilton. Facing the bay and with the Desjardins Marsh behind, this isthmus of land, one hundred feet above the water, was unassailable except across a narrow neck of land bristling with field guns. Legend has it that the Duke of Wellington,

*The Escarpment creeks and the villages where they empty into Lake Ontario are named for their distance from the Niagara River. At Four Mile Creek today is the village of Virgil; at Ten Mile Creek, Homer; at Twelve Mile Creek, St. Catharines; at Twenty Mile Creek, Jordan; at Forty Mile Creek, Grimsby.

studying a map of Upper Canada, put his finger on Burlington Heights as the place he would choose to defend. Here, Vincent would try to hold the British army together against the advancing enemy.

But the militia he did not want. It had been "like drawing their eye teeth" to call them out a month ago, now he did not know how to get rid of them. Lieutenant-Colonel John Harvey writing at Burlington, June 4, to Major Titus G. Simons, commanding the Incorporated Militia, acknowledged that Vincent had had an eye-opener.

> Having witnessed with admiration the gallant conduct of that part of the militia which happened to be in the neighbourhood of Fort George, and which at the moment of attack, instead of diminishing, actually increased to nearly double its numbers by the influx of its brave members who were within reach of the scene of action, ... General Vincent feels that it is only necessary for him to point out to the militia officers and soldiers how they can best under the circumstances promote the cause in which we are engaged to ensure on their part the warmest support and the most cordial co-operation.
>
> It is not by joining us as a military body that your cause can at this moment be best advanced. When our reinforcements have all arrived and all other arrangements matured for repossessing ourselves of the country we have for the moment yielded, and for driving the invader far back into his own settlements, then will the gallant militia of Upper Canada be called upon to join and add inestimable strength in our ranks.

But things would not happen quite that way. The soldiers were as eager to fight as the militia, and Lieutenant-Colonel J. Harvey, working with men like James FitzGibbon, would do something about it. History would call their daring attack the Battle of Stoney Creek.

I wish some of your merchants
would be enterprising enough to
send us up supplies of shoes,
shirts, stockings, &c, &c. Not one
in 20 has an article more than
what is on his person. Adieu.

Lieutenant James FitzGibbon to
the Reverend James Somerville
of Montreal. Burlington Bay,
June 7, 1813.

6

General Vincent was indeed in trouble. For one
thing his army had worn out its shoes. On May 31, he wrote
from Bazeley's farmhouse, Head of the Lake, "We want everything – shoes, stockings, blankets, tents and shirts. I have wrote
to York to forward me all they may have at that post."

Even worse, they lacked ammunition. There were ninety
rounds remaining to each man, and with York fallen to the
enemy and Chauncey's fleet hovering like a bird of prey on Lake
Ontario, there was little hope of getting more. Vincent wrote
Prevost on May 28 from Fort George that he was falling back to
the Head of the Lake with his whole force of 1,600 men. By June
5, the American army of about 2,500, including 250 cavalry and
eight guns, under Generals Chandler and Winder, had reached
Forty Mile Creek (now Grimsby). The British rear guard had
been camping at Stoney Creek near Lake Ontario, about seven
miles from Burlington Heights, and now had to fall back with
the main body on the Heights. Scouts brought the news to Vincent that the Americans were preparing to camp at Stoney
Creek.

History does not agree on who suggested a night attack to Colonel Harvey or on who spied out the American camp. Merritt says the suggestion was made by Coronet McKenney, one of his dragoons, or by Mr. George, an ensign in the militia. And while some sources name Billy Green as the man who visited the American camp, FitzGibbon's granddaughter tells as straightforward fact that it was James FitzGibbon who did the spying. The incident is so in keeping with his madcap courage and the comic streak in his character that it is tempting to believe her.

She says that he volunteered to learn the exact position and disposition of the camp and that he did it by disguising himself as a settler and selling butter to the Americans. Miss Fitz-Gibbon, recalling her grandfather's personality, says, "There is no doubt whatever that he made himself very entertaining to the soldiers, to whom he sold all his butter, getting the best price for it."

FitzGibbon was an excellent storyteller and a born entertainer. Miss FitzGibbon says her grandfather let the Americans think he was giving them much valuable information (all of it erroneous) on the state of affairs in the British camp. In fact, he was seeing and hearing all that the British needed to know about the American camp.

He made his way back to Burlington convinced that a night attack would work. Harvey took the plan to Vincent, and after deliberation, Vincent agreed upon it.

There was little time to lose. In the morning the Americans would attack them and their enemy's superiority in number would force them to flee and abandon the peninsula. Colonel Procter and the whole western country would then fall to the Americans. They had only tonight to change the course of history.

At eleven o'clock, the men, who were already asleep on the grass, were awakened and the march toward the enemy started. A brief shower fell on the men as they started through the pitch dark night.

FitzGibbon was commanding the 5th company from the head of the column. He says they had about 700 men, Merritt says

590. When they were three miles out, the march was stopped and the men were told they were undertaking a night attack. At this point the loading was drawn from each man's gun.

FitzGibbon knew as he withdrew the flint from his gun that this would cost lives. Men would have to stand under enemy fire and concentrate on the awkward task of replacing a flint. Many would fall without succeeding. But it had to be. James knew very well the excitable Irish temperament of these "green tigers." It would take only one man with a flint in his gun to fire too soon to bring disaster upon them all.

Fitz talked to his company, explaining what lay ahead and urging them to depend on the vicious silence of the bayonet. He could feel the tense awareness in his men, the controlled fear, the readiness to face death in the dark tonight rather than wait for poorer odds tomorrow. The march went on, eastward along Burlington Bay. It was good to turn your face toward Fort George, even in the black of night. It was nearly two o'clock in the warm, damp, silent night when the ghost-like column of moving men neared Stoney Creek. The enforced quiet had drawn nerves taut.

In a diagram drawn later by FitzGibbon, the Americans are shown camped in Gage's fields at the foot of a twenty-foot hill, 500 of them to the left of the land leading to Gage's house, 2,000 on the right. Their guns were on the brow of the hill, positioned in the road. Pickets were half a mile ahead in the woods. The first two sentries were made prisoners silently. The third resisted and was bayoneted. His cries alerted the men of the next picket at the entrance to the cleared field and one of them fired a shot. By now the first two companies of the column were upon the 500. Surprise was complete until suddenly the officers in front began cheering. The soldiers took up the cry, the tension of their silent march broken, absolute bedlam resulting. Fitz-Gibbon was furious:

> I was aware that it would be almost impossible to make the men silent again, and that consequently orders could not be heard or obeyed. I instantly turned to my men and charged them not to take up the shout then coming from the front, and by the assistance of my three sergeants, I succeeded in

keeping them silent and in good order until a late stage of the affair, when firing on our side became general. Then, shouting, we rushed into the open ground occupied by the enemy and wheeled to the left.

The surprised Americans ran from their campfires to the hill behind them. Soon the 2,000 on the right of the road opened a tremendous fire upon the British soldiers who were "endeavoring to form in extreme darkness upon unknown and rough ground covered with rail fences, fallen trees and stumps." Still worse, they were lighted by the campfires of the Americans while the Americans were an unseen enemy firing out of the darkness on the hill.

Our men never ceased shouting. No order could be heard. Everything was noise and confusion – which confusion was chiefly occasioned by the noise. Our men returned fire contrary to orders and it soon became apparent that it was impossible to prevent shouting and firing. The scene at this instant was awfully grand. The darkness of the morning, 2 o'clock, [was] made still more dark by the flashing of the musketry and cannon. The officers could no longer control their men and they soon began to fall back.

Suddenly Major Plenderleath of the 49th decided on charging the guns that were firing down the road upon them. With part of FitzGibbon's company and a few other men, he rushed the guns and took all four of them. The two American generals, Chandler and Winder, rushed forward and Plenderleath's party made prisoners of them. As well, they took five field officers and captains and one hundred other prisoners. The Americans, finding the British at the top of the hill right in their centre, broke and fled. Just in time, for the British were fleeing, too. The total confusion and the terror of night fighting had almost finished them. Fitz said, "I am of the opinion that had not Major Plenderleath made the dash he did the Americans would have kept their ground and our ruin would have been inevitable."

Daylight comes early to Stoney Creek in June, and daylight would reveal to the Americans how few soldiers made up this screaming, cheering hell that had attacked them in the night.

Colonel Harvey prudently withdrew his men from the field in the last shreds of darkness.

General Vincent was lost. Harvey sent William Hamilton Merritt to search for him among the dead and wounded strewn for two miles along the road and woods. Challenged by an American sentry near Gage's house, Merritt almost became a prisoner. But his blue jacket let him pretend he was one of them, and by this ruse he took the American prisoner instead, then captured a second who came up. But he found no Vincent, either dead or alive. FitzGibbon, who rarely speaks well of Vincent, says, "General Vincent with the whole left of the line retreated, or I may say fled into the woods, and not until noon next day did we know what was become of him. A flag of truce was sent to inquire if he was taken but the Americans knew nothing of him. Indians were sent in search of him but without success. He at length found a road and joined us. Numbers of officers and men were lost for a time in the woods, so difficult is it to navigate these forests."

On the morning of the sixth, the grim work of carrying away the wounded and burying the dead in Gage's fields went on. Many of the dead buried by British soldiers were American.

Two thousand more Americans had been landed by Chauncey's ships on the lake shore the evening before, and during the day they made their way to the now-deserted battlefield. They burnt whatever was not yet carried off by the British, wagons loaded with flour, arms and appointments and other camp equipage. Then they joined their main body now falling back to Forty Mile Creek.

By the seventh, the Indians had heard what was happening and Merritt says "they came on in droves." The militia, who had been sent home frustrated by Vincent, now saw their chance and swarmed out again to make prisoners of those Americans who were still lost in the woods. At six o'clock on the seventh, the Americans at Forty Mile Creek thought they saw Chauncey's sails appear on the silver sheet of Lake Ontario. There was great rejoicing until they could make out the flags. Then dismay! Those ships were British! Sir James Yeo had set sail from Kingston on June 3 and was making his first public appearance before a large, unappreciative American audience. Prevost had already led him to attack Sackett's Harbour while the American fleet attacked Fort George, but nothing decisive had been accomplished there. Although he could not bring his ships close to the shore, he was sending his gunboats in with a sharp and well-directed fire against the batteries the Americans had set up. Meanwhile Indians had taken up a position on the escarpment behind the Americans to discomfit them even more.

On the eighth, Yeo sent in a note demanding the surrender of the American army, and the Americans decided on a full retreat by land to Fort George. They tried to send some baggage and camp equipment by bateaux but seventeen of these were captured by a British schooner. Mostly they just left it all behind.

When Lieutenant-Colonel Bisshopp's advance party arrived, they found 500 tents still standing, 140 barrels of flour, 100 stand of arms, a considerable amount of other stores, and seventy prisoners. He did not say whether they found any shoes for the ragged British army.

Afterwards, people on the Niagara Peninsula would tell how it took the Americans four days to make their way up to Stoney Creek, less than one day to run back.

A wonderful change has taken
place in our prospects since the
nocturnal visit to the enemy's encampment at Stoney Creek on
the 6th. We begin to carry on our
arrangements as usual. We are all
well and in the highest spirits.

Major J.B. Glegg to William Jarvis, Forty Mile Creek, June 15,
1813.

7

In the midst of all the rejoicing ("a Royal Salute was
fired in Kingston in celebration of the splendid achievement"),
James FitzGibbon was not satisfied. His granddaughter says he
always believed that the British should have pursued the retreating Americans. They might have recovered Fort George
with little loss. Nor did the exploit at Stoney Creek suit his
fancy.

In his letter to the Rev. James Somerville in Montreal he
writes: "This affair is much praised and the Americans think it a
brilliant one on our part, but for myself it is an evidence most
convincing of the deficiency of our officers in general." What infuriated FitzGibbon was the officers' shouting and giving themselves away before they had formed their line to attack.

> Never was surprise more complete – never was anything
> more brilliant than it would have been had we kept silence
> and not fired, but our officers began that which they should
> have watched with all their care to prevent; for they ought
> to have known that in darkness and noise confusion must
> be inevitable. I think I could have killed some of them had I
> been near them at the moment.

Already in his mind, Fitz was developing guerrilla tactics. The woods of Canada called for new methods of stealth and cunning. He admired and learned from the Indians and from militiamen like W.H. Merritt, who knew this territory, and used their knowledge to outwit the Americans. He felt closer to them than he did to his British superiors for he was fed up with procrastination and with hide-bound methods of defence and attack. He wanted desperately to do something impulsive and personal.

Fourteen years before in his first major battle at Egmont-op-Zee in Holland, FitzGibbon had decided the best place to be in any battle was out in front. That day he had watched Savery Brock, a brother of Isaac Brock, lead the men from one sand hill to another, always in front in the thick of enemy fire.

> A large man so exposed – I watched from moment to moment to see him fall, but for about two hours while in my view he remained untouched.
>
> After witnessing Savery Brock's conduct, I determined to be the first to advance every time at the head of those around me, and I soon saw that of those who were most prompt to follow me, fewer fell by the enemy's fire than I witnessed falling of those more in our rear.

Right now, on June 6, 1813, he had to find some way to be out in front, not five columns back in the noise and confusion. What if he had fifty men to command in advance, to use in the woods as he saw fit? He went to Lieutenant-Colonel Harvey with his idea. Harvey told him to be back within an hour with a detailed plan of operation which he would take to General Vincent. Vincent, probably persuaded by Harvey, approved.

According to his granddaughter, the whole 49th Regiment wanted to join FitzGibbon's band. She quotes an old 49th man, writing in 1860: "We all wanted to go. We knew there would be good work, fighting and success wherever FitzGibbon led, for though impulsive he was prompt, and as brave as a lion. Though apparently foolhardy, every man in the regiment knew that he knew what he was about, and forgot nothing."

Ensign Winder was his first choice. The other forty-eight rank and file came from the different companies of the 49th. Each man was already a "green tiger" in the jargon of the army, although this nickname was most often used by Americans to describe their fear of the 49ers. In battle after battle "those damned green tigers" would charge them with bayonets or storm their guns. Usually in the front of every fight, they were often the irresistible force that broke and scattered the blue American line. Now, with fifty of their best men hand-picked and organized into a fast-moving, horse-riding band of holy-terrors, the name Green Tiger would take on new menace and many an American would wish he had never crossed the Niagara frontier.

Somewhere FitzGibbon managed to get enough cloth to have fifty grey jackets made as well as fifty red ones; the grey ones were camouflage ("Grey, being the nearest to the colour of the bark on the forest trees, is least discernible"). Sometimes he would use the jackets alternately to look like twice his numbers. He also bought three cow-bells to be used for signals at night although he says he never actually used them.

He divided his fifty men into three parties, each in the charge of a sergeant, and began moving them, not by main roads, but by Indian paths and escarpment trails, into territory where American raiding parties were robbing the farmers, terrorizing their wives, and taking old men prisoners. His assignment was to stop these assaults. He was also to collect information on the enemy's movements and do everything in his power to annoy the American army.

Working with him in similar style was William Hamilton Merritt and his provincial dragoons. A group of them under Coronet McKenney were attached directly to FitzGibbon's party. British soldier and militiaman alike were delighted to be pushing again toward Fort George.

Lieutenant-Colonel Harvey in a letter from Forty Mile Creek, June 11, 1813, explains General Vincent's plan for the Niagara frontier and expresses Vincent's new admiration for the militia and yeomanry. (Harvey himself, an able, intelligent young man who later became governor of Nova Scotia, probably deserves credit for the better liaison and understanding between British officer and Niagara farmer.)

> The principal objects General Vincent has had in view in making a forward movement with the greatest part of the troops to this place are to communicate and give every support and assistance in his power to Sir James Yeo and the fleet and be at hand to take advantage of the success which we sanguinely anticipate from the approaching encounter with Commodore Chauncey, to give encouragement to the militia and yeomanry of the country, who are everywhere rising upon the fugitive Americans and making them prisoners, and withholding all supplies from them, and lastly (and perhaps chiefly) for the purpose of sparing the resources of the country in our rear and drawing the supplies of this army, as long as possible, from the country in the enemy's vicinity. Our position here secures all these important objects, and so long as our fleet is triumphant it is a secure one. Should any disaster (which God forbid) befall that we have no longer any business *here* or in this part of *Canada*.

If Sir James Yeo could handle Chauncey on the water, the British army, with men like FitzGibbon and Merritt out in front, could pin the Americans inside Fort George. They might have to do it barefoot and half-clad, substituting a lot of spirit for a lack of supplies. On June 14 Vincent wrote to Colonel Baynes again about shoes, "I have to request shoes may be sent. We are more in want of them than any other article." On June 18 Captain James P. Fulton wrote to Sir George Prevost, "On my arrival here I found the troops in great distress for necessaries, shirts, shoes and stockings. Most of the 49th are *literally* naked." The food situation was also becoming difficult. On June 10, Vincent sent all women and children belonging to the corps in Upper Canada to Montreal by bateaux. No rations were to be issued to soldiers' wives unless they were to serve as nurses. Sir James Yeo made a foray to the mouth of the Genessee River and captured all the provisions found in the government stores as well as a sloop laden with grain. This would help, but Vincent knew that all the rich resources of the Niagara Peninsula must be regained to keep his army fed.

By June 16, FitzGibbon was perched in a bold position at DeCew's, seven miles inland from the army's advance post at the mouth of the Twelve where Major De Haren was in command with 200 of the 104th Regiment and 300 Caughnawagas newly arrived from Lower Canada. Colonel Cecil Bisshopp with a larger force waited at Twenty Mile Creek. Vincent with the main body of the British army was back at the Forty. The DeCew position put FitzGibbon at the point of a triangle, seven miles from Major De Haren and about ten miles from Colonel Bisshopp. It was an ideal position from which to swoop out in any direction and in particular to take the Mountain Road through St. David's to Queenston and intercept the communication between Fort George and Fort Erie.

Mrs. DeCew and her children crowded into one or two rooms upstairs while FitzGibbon's fifty men, when they had time to eat or sleep, used the downstairs. Mrs. DeCew had a grand house with large fireplaces and walls finished in black walnut inside and fruit trees around the outside. But John DeCew was a prisoner in the United States, carried off by one of the raiding parties which plagued the countryside after Fort George fell. His wife was delighted to harbour and help these "wild Irishmen" who might stop Chapin's "vagabonds."

Dr. Cyrenius Chapin was the most hated man on the Niagara frontier. He commanded a troop of mounted men who would swoop down on Niagara farmers, taking prisoners and plundering property. A doctor from Buffalo, he thought he was saving the Canadian settlers from British tyranny, but FitzGibbon and his men were determined to save the settlers from the terror of Chapin.

His granddaughter tells a story that demonstrates the quick, calculated thinking and the wild sense of humour that made FitzGibbon so suited to his type of warfare. On one of his forays into the woods, he and two men met ten or twelve Americans almost head-on. An overhanging bank of earth with a tangle of wild vines gave them a hiding place in the nick of time. The

Americans had been following a path which ended here on the top of this bluff and now were unsure which way to go. Fitz-Gibbon signalled his men to remain still, and they watched him creep along the bank toward a cave they knew about. A large fallen tree blocked the cave's entrance. They watched Fitz-Gibbon use his hands to pivot himself silently over it, at the same time getting a look at the enemy above him. Suddenly, an incredible bedlam of Indian war whoops and wild Irish yells broke loose. FitzGibbon was using the reverberations in the cave to sound like a horde of Indians and a pack of Green Tigers. Terrified, believing themselves ambushed, the Americans turned and fled. The two men under the vines could hear feet pounding above them. They added some wild cries to the banshee voices of their leader and then, as FitzGibbon emerged from the cave, his face lit up with glee, all three dissolved into well-earned laughter.

But it wasn't all a lark. The prolonged tension and lack of decent rest and food must have often worn them weary and gaunt. Merritt says that FitzGibbon never slept twice in the same place. Charles Askin writing to his father, the fur-trader John Askin, called Fitz, "one of the most active and pleasing officers we have," and said that he was "flying about in such a manner that the enemy did not know where to find him."

Typical of the pace he kept was a sortie made on June 21 that same summer. With Merritt, McKenney, Cummings, and young Barnard, staff adjutant to Colonel Bisshopp, he was sent to Point Abino on Lake Erie to bring back a Mr. Tyce Horn (Haun) who was helping the Americans. All the country from Chippawa to Fort Erie was in American hands. At one place they were nearly fired on by Canadians who were "sulking from the Americans." Chapin was in the area, had passed down an hour before. They would have to consider the possibility of meeting him on the river road when they returned. It had turned cold and started to rain. The rain continued all night. It was two o'clock when they reached Horn's house and surrounded it. They were so cold they could hardly dismount from their horses. They took Horn and one of Chapin's men prisoners and in spite of their chilled condition, started the long ride back. Merritt says he was back at the Twelve by nine the next morning, and went on to the Forty to make out muster rolls, etc. against the 24th. He doesn't say whether FitzGibbon got home to DeCew's for a rest, or went on to his next escapade.

One June day, Fitz received the only wound of his career. He had been walking noiselessly through the bush and stopped a moment to lean against a tree. Suddenly he felt the presence of another person and turned in time to see a man fire at him. Fitz felt the ball strike him and he staggered. But seconds later he was chasing the man. The man fell, dropped his rifle, and Fitz grabbed him. Winder had heard the shot and came running up. Between them they took the man prisoner.

For two days FitzGibbon was bruised, stiff, and sore. The prisoner was heard to tell people no bullet would kill "that damned Green Tiger" for he had certainly hit him. FitzGibbon began to wonder himself why he wasn't dead. He and Winder went back to look and found that the ball had first gone through a young tree. That and the thickness of his coat and the fact that he had turned in the nick of time, probably saved his life.

Many years later, in a letter to his youngest son who was receiving his first commission in the 24th Regiment, FitzGibbon passed on "advice for his guidance in woody warfare," knowledge garnered from these days of bush fighting in 1813 and 1814. "The troops should be drilled in the woods. The soldier should face to the right of the tree; thus a very small section of his head and right arm and shoulder is exposed. ... The soldier, when advancing, should not go straight forward, but at an angle to some tree to the right or left of the one he quits."

His admiration for the skill of the Indians is evident again when he said, "I recommend that an intelligent Indian be attached to each regiment for a sufficient time to teach all his lessons ... to the officers and sergeants. ... One of the most efficient means of winning the highest degree of the soldier's goodwill and confidence is by carefully keeping him out of every unnecessary danger, and often going yourself to reconnoitre, rather than to send another to do so."

One of FitzGibbon's particular interests was the physical fitness of his soldiers. "Let them run races, jump, leap, wrestle, use the pike, sword, stick, cricket-bat, quoits, as each may desire or you direct. Swimming should also be practised." Another of his favourite themes was fighting at night: "I think fighting at night has never been practised to one-tenth of the extent to which it is possible to carry it out." Speaking of his band in 1813, he said, "I had men who could rejoice in being able to accomplish what other men would not think of even attempting."

Above all, Fitz said, an officer needed to have, "knowledge of the comparative qualities of those he commands and those to whom he is opposed." He always saw two opposing armies as possessing, "a certain quantum of courage and confidence, usually unequally divided and always liable to fluctuation." It was up to an officer, "to so play his game that he shall from day to day and from one affair to another win from his adversary's scales more or less of these qualities, and transfer the gain to his own scales." This was the distillation of all his learning and experience, but in 1813 he was still in the school of very hard knocks.

By June 20, he and Chapin were determined to get at each other. Fitz knew that Chapin, who did most of his raiding from Fort Erie to Chippawa, was in the area of Fort George. Fitz-Gibbon's Green Tigers dispersed through the woods to locate him and a group of them removed the planks from the Chippawa Bridge to keep Chapin's forty-nine men from fleeing home to Buffalo when they closed in on him. FitzGibbon's Tigers thought they had him until it was discovered that 150 American infantrymen from Fort Erie had also come over the bridge before they removed the planks.

Fitz had his men gathered in Lundy's Lane ready to ambush Chapin's forty-nine at Forsyth's woods near the Falls. He had come on ahead into the small village to reconnoitre. Suddenly Mrs. Kirby, who lived on the corner, ran out waving at him to go back.

"There are two or three hundred men with Chapin and they just this moment passed by. For goodness sake," she pleaded, "go back!"

But FitzGibbon had spied an American horse by Deffield's Inn and, assuming there was only one American inside, decided to take him. He rode over, dismounted, and entered the inn where he found not one American but two, a rifleman and a soldier. FitzGibbon soon had a rifle pointed at him. He summoned all his Irish charm and pretended to be an old acquaintance. This put the Americans off their guard for an instant. Merritt says Fitz proffered one hand in greeting and with the other seized the rifle. "The soldier was in the act of firing when he fortunately caught his gun, brought both of them under his arm, by which means the muzzles of each were pointing at his comrade, both cocked, the friction of the two enabled him to keep them so firm that they could not with every exertion break his grasp. In this position he pulled and pushed them both out of the house, the steps of which were two or three feet high, he swearing and demanding them to surrender, they retorting the demand on him."

The *Montreal Gazette*, which had discovered the romance and drama of FitzGibbon's little band, got the story three weeks later, and they told it this way:

> In this situation Lieut. F. called upon two men who were looking on to assist him in disarming the two Americans, but they would not interfere. Poor Mrs. Kirby, apparently distracted, used all her influence, but in vain. The rifleman finding that he could not disengage his piece, drew Lieut. F's sword out of his scabbard with his left hand with the intention of striking at Lieut. F., when another woman, Mrs. Danfield [Deffield?], seized the uplifted arm and wrested the sword from his grasp. At this moment an elderly man, named Johnson, came up and forced the American from his hold on the rifle, and Lieut. F. immediately laid the other soldier prostrate.

Merritt says Fitz got on his horse, led the other horse and drove the two gentlemen before him to his party. "He had not left the place two minutes before the [American] party returned. Upon the whole it was a most gallant, daring and miraculous proceeding."

Whenever Fitz had to talk about the incident he said he had been plain foolish. Looking back in later years, Fitz must have wondered whether he had not done a lot of plain foolish things but miraculously he had got away with them all. Tiger was an apt name to describe him. He was a cat with nine lives, nimble, lithe, quick, and cool. He was no hero, although he was about to become one that June. He and Doctor Cyrenius Chapin were about to meet at the Beaver Dam where he would stake one of his nine lives to win fame and promotion at the Battle of Beaver Dam. At the same time a woman named Laura Secord would gain immortal fame.

And when the Yankees *did* surrender, we all wondered what the
mischief he [FitzGibbon] would
do with them.

Judge Jarvis of Brockville, who
was with FitzGibbon at Beaver
Dam.

8

One of the best-known tales of Canadian history
concerns the woman who walked twenty miles to warn James
FitzGibbon that the Americans were coming to get him. In the
telling, facts have often been altered, and embellishments added.
Someone put a cow in the story and it has been hard to get it out.
Then the woman herself, clad in a lacy bonnet, became forever
associated with a delicious brand of chocolates, giving the whole
story quite a special flavour.

But the facts themselves are really quite remarkable. They are
plainly written on her monument in Drummond Hill Cemetery,
Lundy's Lane, Niagara Falls, where Laura lies buried:

To Perpetuate
The Name and Fame of
LAURA SECORD

who walked alone nearly 20 miles by a
circuitous, difficult and perilous
route, through woods and swamps and
over miry roads, to warn a British

outpost at DeCew's Falls, of an
intended attack, and thereby enabled
Lieut. FitzGibbon on the 24 June 1813
with less than 50 men of H.M. 49th
Regiment, about 15 militia men, and a
small force of Six Nation and other
Indians under Captains William Johnson
Kerr and Dominique Ducharme, to surprise
and attack the enemy at Beechwoods (or
Beaver Dams) and after a short engage-
ment to capture Col. Boerstler of the
U.S. Army and his entire force of 542
men with 2 field pieces.

James and Laura Secord's house, which can still be seen today, sat under the shadow of Queenston Heights. Portage (or River) Road came down the Heights running close to the Secord house and along it clattered all the "going and coming" of whichever army held Fort George. The windows of the house looked toward the Niagara River and the Queenston Wharf where the Americans landed in October 1812. On that October day, less than a year before, General Brock had died on the Heights above Laura's home, and her husband James had been badly wounded. Laura herself had gone to the Heights, searched among the dying for her husband and with the help of "a Gentleman" got him down the hill into their own house.

She found that their house, from which she had fled with her small children at dawn, was a wreck now, plundered by the Americans. Laura swallowed her tears and anger as she made her husband a bed in a corner of the chaos. Afterwards she took James and their children to spend the winter with relatives in St. David's, three miles west of Queenston. In June of 1813, Queenston was still at the mercy of the Americans, and James was still unwell from the wounds in his shoulder and knee, but the Secords were back at their own hearth. Portage Road was an American thoroughfare these days although it made James grin with pride to see FitzGibbon's or Merritt's horsemen dash along it now and again on some surreptitious errand.

Laura never knew when Americans would knock on her door and demand lodging or food. When they did she had to comply.

Laura herself did not put in writing exactly how she learned of the plan to capture FitzGibbon, but legend and her grandchildren agree that Americans taking food in her home revealed the scheme. Laura's granddaughter, Laura Secord Clark, says that Laura gave them food and liquor, then listened outside the window.

It was Cyrenius Chapin who started the agitation to "get Fitz-Gibbon." He and Fitz had been playing cat and mouse for over a month, and Chapin now had a scheme to decide finally who was the cat. While FitzGibbon and his friends were riding to Point Abino to capture Tyce Horn, Chapin was on his way to Fort George with his plan in his head. He would convince Lieutenant-Colonel Boerstler that he had spied out the route to DeCew's, that he could guide him there with 500 men and take the fifty British and close to one hundred Indians, with ease.

It is quite possible that on that wet and unseasonably cold June 21, when FitzGibbon and Merritt on their way to Point Abino heard of Chapin passing down an hour before, Chapin and his men would have stopped at the Secord house before riding on another seven miles to Fort George. It is easy to picture them, warmed by food and drink, leaning back in their chairs to talk and laugh about what they would do to FitzGibbon.

Laura Secord knew how important FitzGibbon was to the frontier. Without his band and Merritt's dragoons they would be entirely under the American thumb. Her half-brother, Charles Ingersoll, was a lieutenant in William Hamilton Merritt's Niagara Provincial Light Dragoons; Laura often heard of Fitz-Gibbon from him. When the Americans had gone, she told her husband what she had heard, and added, "Somebody has to warn FitzGibbon." Her crippled husband remarked wryly that if he crawled on his hands and knees he could not get there in time. Laura thought of Chapin at Fort George preparing disaster for the men at DeCew's. She had no idea how quickly the Americans might move out. She made her decision. She herself would go.

Actually Chapin was having some problems at Fort George

with his own superior officer. Lieutenant-Colonel Charles Boerstler was a man who had no respect for Doctor Chapin. He did have a healthy respect for the British army and for Lieutenant FitzGibbon's Green Tigers. He was not at all convinced that Chapin knew the roads and trails and swamps and positions of the British well enough to get him to DeCew's – and back alive. But it seems that Chapin got through to a higher authority. Brigadier-General John P. Boyd was the American officer in charge at Fort George. On June 23, Boyd gave Charles Boerstler orders to take 500 men to DeCew's house and capture or wipe out the enemy stationed there. He was to march his men to Queenston in the evening and reach DeCew's the following day. Boerstler was shocked, but he got the operation under way.

Meanwhile Laura had left the house at 4:30 in the morning on June 22. As the story is told by FitzGibbon's granddaughter, Laura pretended to be trying to catch a cow to milk it when an American sentry questioned her. But Laura's biographer, Ruth Mackenzie, says there was no cow and probably no sentry either. Anyway, Laura had another excuse for being abroad so early. She would tell any American she met that she was on her way to visit her brother Charles, lying sick of a fever at Hannah Secord's house near St. David's. (Charles was engaged to marry Hannah's daughter, Elizabeth.)

Charles was still sick in bed. Laura may have hoped that he would help her with the message but he was unable to get up. Elizabeth Secord offered to go with Laura. The two women set out. Afraid of American patrols on the Mountain Road to Beaver Dam, they took the Old Swamp Road west to Shipman's Corners (St. Catharines), then turned south to DeCew's. This way led over miry roads made worse by the all-night rain, through sloughs and muddy swamp that tugged at their feet and slowed their pace. They were often in the shadow of deep woods where mosquitoes rose in clouds to add to their misery. When not in the shade of trees, the day was becoming excessively hot.

At Shipman's Corners, Elizabeth had to quit and stay at the home of a friend. She was unwell and had only a year to live. Laura, although she looked frail, was strong and tough. But as she went on alone, she was afraid. Every woman she had encountered along the way had warned her of the dangers from the Indians. There were hundreds of them encamped in these woods, they had said, and no woman was safe among them. Laura, marching on, told herself the Indians were friends to the British and the stories of their atrocities much exaggerated. If only she knew this territory better. The hills and ravines and passes through the valleys confused her, and she kept taking the wrong trails. It was uphill, too, as she was actually climbing the escarpment. And the day was wearing on to the edge of darkness. She was almost too tired to think, too exhausted to walk. Suddenly she found herself surrounded by Indians.

All the sensible things she had kept telling herself about the Indians gave way to complete terror and she could not speak. But the authority of their chief in quieting the others reassured her. She was able to make him understand that the Americans were coming, that she had to talk to FitzGibbon. Finally the chief volunteered to go with her to DeCew's house.

When they arrived James FitzGibbon was more than a little surprised to hear the story of this frail little woman who claimed to have walked from Queenston. Queenston was twenty miles distant by the Old Swamp Road. But her obvious fatigue, her bedraggled appearance, and the urgency in her voice, made it impossible to doubt her.

"Mrs. Secord," he wrote later, "was a person of slight and delicate frame and made this effort in weather excessively warm, and I dreaded at the time that she must suffer in health in consequence of fatigue and anxiety, she having been exposed to danger from the enemy, through whose line of communication she had to pass."

FitzGibbon sent her to Turney's farm at the Crossroads beyond DeCew's where, as she expressed it later, she "slept right off."

FitzGibbon could not tell how much time he had. He sent a message to Colonel Bisshopp and Major De Haren but he realized he might have to act without them. There were 400 Indians at the Beaver Dam, about two miles east of DeCew's house. One hundred eighty of these were Caughnawagas, newly arrived from Lower Canada under a militia captain, Dominique Ducharme. Captain William Kerr had 200 from the Six Nations, mostly Mohawks, and there were eighty from various other tribes. By night time he had the Indians posted in a good position to intercept the Americans and Fitz stayed on guard during the night. In the morning he sent Captain Ducharme to reconnoitre. Ducharme went all the way to the Niagara River, got into a battle with a small party of Americans, killed four and took seven prisoners. But he saw nothing of 500 marching men.

On the following morning Ducharme's scouts did discover the Americans on the move. Boerstler's little army had spent the night of June 23 in Queenston, throwing out patrols and pickets to prevent any citizen carrying the news. Early the next morning they marched out, confident that surprise was on their side.

The Americans were near their destination, hot and weary from the march, when the beechwoods on either side of them came to life with savage yells and rifle fire. Several cavalrymen, riding rearguard, fell from their horses. Indians appeared on the road behind them cutting off the possibility of retreat. Near the front of the long column Colonel Boerstler was shot in the thigh. Major Taylor, second in command, had his horse shot from under him. Captain Chapin ran to hide behind the ammunition wagons, to the intense fury of Boerstler. Not only had Chapin forced him into this desperate attempt, he had admitted en route that he did not know the roads so that Boerstler had to force a settler to guide his troops; now Cyrenius Chapin was hiding from the enemy.

The fire from the woods was incessant, the Americans could find no escape from it. They attempted to charge the Indians to drive them into an open field, but Boerstler found his men not equal to the Indians in woodland warfare, and they had to fall back. FitzGibbon, who had watched from a high hill to the right of the road, kept careful calculation of the despair and panic in the American ranks. When he thought the moment was right, he rode up with a white handkerchief tied to his sword, while his bugler sounded a *Cease Fire* to the Indians. The beechwoods became still.

FitzGibbon had used bluff before this to get out of a tricky situation, but these were higher odds than he usually played for.

Could he make 500 regular soldiers surrender to his fifty Green Tigers and some Indians they could not see?

British reinforcements had arrived, he said, wishing that they had, and the Indians were becoming hard to control, especially the western ones. In order to avoid bloodshed he must urge the Americans to surrender. Boerstler said he would not surrender to a force he had not even seen. Fitz swallowed hard and said he would ask his superior officer if he might allow one of Boerstler's officers to inspect the British troops.

The only British troops Fitz had, apart from his own Green Tigers, were twenty dragoons who had galloped up under Captain Hall of Chippawa. He also did not have any "superior officer." But maybe Hall would do. "You be my superior officer," he told Hall, "receive the request and refuse it."

Boerstler sent Lieutenant Goodwin to Hall who refused the "humiliation" of having his troops inspected. Boerstler then sent Captain McDowell to ask that he be given until sundown to decide on surrender. (It was about noon.)

FitzGibbon replied, "I cannot possibly grant such a request. I could not control the Indians for such a length of time. I cannot give your general more than five minutes in which to decide whether to surrender or not."

Boerstler's decision was to surrender. He was seventeen miles from Fort George with no hope of reinforcements. He had no idea how many British troops or Indians opposed him. A seventeen-mile retreat with exhausted men at the mercy of the Indians was unthinkable. FitzGibbon promised them protection from the Indians and personally spoke with each of the chiefs, extracting promises from them.

As FitzGibbon was about to accept the surrender of the troops, Major De Haren galloped up from Twenty Mile Creek, prepared to take over. FitzGibbon's temper flared. He knew the prize he had here, and he had worked too hard for the British cause to have his glory snatched away. In an age when officers were usually wealthy men who could afford to purchase their commissions (Isaac Brock had paid $15,000 to rise from Ensign to Lieutenant-Colonel in thirteen years) James FitzGibbon had gone into debt to buy his commission as Ensign in 1806 and not been out of debt since. Promotion would mean increased pay as well as a chance to rise further from the ranks. He needed both.

Grabbing De Haren's horse, he said in an emphatic whisper, "Not another word, sir; not another word; these men are my prisoners." Then stepping back, he asked, "Shall I proceed to disarm the American troops?"

De Haren answered, "You may."

FitzGibbon formed the Americans in file to keep their ranks broken, fearing De Haren might reveal the scarcity of British troops. (FitzGibbon doesn't say how far away De Haren's companies were but they had not yet put in an appearance.) Keeping the Americans apart from his handful of British soldiers, he asked De Haren, "Shall the American troops ground their arms here?"

"No, let them march through between our men and ground their arms on the other side."

FitzGibbon turned a wicked glare on De Haren. Did the man not realize that with a close look at their tiny British force, the Americans might not ground their arms at all? In desperation, Fitz said, "Do you think it prudent to march them through with arms in their hands in the presence of the Indians?"

Boerstler saved the day for FitzGibbon. "For God's sake, sir," he exclaimed, "do what this officer bids you."

"Do so," said De Haren.

But the moment the American soldiers put down their arms, Indians sprang forward. The terrified men began to seize their arms again. Fitz jumped upon a tree stump and shouted, "Americans, don't touch your arms! Not a hair on your head shall be hurt. Remember, I am here." A bombastic speech, he admitted afterwards, but the chiefs had given him their promise and he believed them. The Indians helped themselves to pistols, swords, and jackets that pleased them, contrary to the terms of capitulation, but none of them inflicted physical harm. At last FitzGibbon could relax. De Haren requested him to conduct Colonel Boerstler to DeCew's house.

As they rode the two miles together, FitzGibbon discovered he liked this man Boerstler. The wound in his leg looked painful but he rode without complaining. He had been caught in a vicious trap, the victim of poor planning by his superior officers, poor guidance by Chapin, and betrayal by a woman whose long walk FitzGibbon would keep secret to protect her throughout the rest of the war. Colonel Boerstler would go home to face a court of enquiry but its final verdict would be that his personal deportment "was that of a brave, zealous and deliberate officer, and the conduct of the regular officers and men under his command was equally honorable to themselves and to their country."

Chapin was a prisoner of the British at last but he proved a hard man to hold on to. On July 12, he and twenty-eight of his men were sent east to Kingston under a guard of sixteen soldiers in two boats. At a signal from Chapin his men in the other boat drew along side and boarded the boat Chapin was in. In the struggle Chapin's men overpowered their guard, turned their boats back, and landed the next day at Fort George. Chapin kept his freedom until the end of December when he was again taken prisoner at Buffalo; this time the British managed to convey him, with no mistakes, to a Quebec jail.

Meanwhile FitzGibbon's performance would catch the imagination of the Canadas and he would become the "hero of Beaver Dam."

9

The *Montreal Gazette* had already learned that the exploits of James FitzGibbon made good copy, and they were quick to pick up his latest adventure. They had the story by the 6th of July: "We have much satisfaction in communicating to the public the particulars of a campaign not of a *General* with his *thousands* but of a *lieutenant* with his *tens* only." The story went on to talk of "the cool determination and the hardy presence of mind evinced by this highly meritorious officer," and to suggest that "the brilliant result which crowned these exertions will, while they make known to the world the name of Lieutenant FitzGibbon, reflect new lustre if possible, on the well-earned reputation of the gallant 49th Regt., and class that event with the most extraordinary occurrences of the present accursed war."

As a result of the battle at Beaver Dam, FitzGibbon was promoted to Captain in the Glengarry Light Infantry Fencibles. However, he was to stay with his band of the 49th for the rest of the campaign in that year, 1813.

The Indians under Dominique Ducharme were not satisfied that enough of the official credit went to them. Merritt quotes a comment by Captain Norton which describes their feelings: "The *Cognawaga* [*sic*] *Indians* fought the *battle*, the *Mohawks* or Six Nations got the *plunder*, and *FitzGibbon* got the *credit*." When the war was over the controversy continued. On March 30, 1818, FitzGibbon put his position on paper: "With respect to the affair with Captain Boerstler, not a shot was fired on our side by any but the Indians. They beat the American detachment into a state of terror, and the only share I claim is taking advantage of a favourable moment to offer them protection from the tomahawk and scalping knife. The Indian department did all the rest."

Actually the promotion given FitzGibbon may have been due not entirely to Boerstler's capture but also to his service with the Green Tigers. Colonel Baynes wrote to Sir George Prevost on July 1: "I beg strongly to recommend to your Excellency's notice the pretensions of Lieut. FitzGibbon of the 49th, from the circumstances above stated, but most particularly from his ability as an officer of a light corps, in which line of service he has recently so eminently distinguished himself."

The real significance of the affair was its effect on the Americans. President Madison ordered General Dearborn to resign shortly after the Boerstler fiasco, and the command of the American army went to Generals Boyd and Lewis. For the rest of the summer the Americans kept 4,000 men cooped up inside Fort George. James J. Fulton, aide-de-camp to Sir George Prevost, writing on June 28, said, "Indeed, from anything we learn since Colonel Boerstler's disaster, they have not dared to send a patrol more than one mile from Fort George in any direction."

The British, infused with new spirit, pressed closer. At the end of June, Vincent moved his whole army (about 1,800 men) up to the Twelve Mile Creek. On the first of July the advanced posts of the army were pushed on to St. David's. Soldiers, militiamen, and Indians were all in a mood to take the offensive. No one was more eager to get on with the action than James Fitz-Gibbon. On July 4, he had Ensign Winder organize a party of seven Green Tigers, thirty-four militiamen and one volunteer, to cross the Niagara in three boats and attack Fort Schlosser opposite Chippawa. It was the night of Independence Day and FitzGibbon had calculated to catch the Americans off guard. Winder took the guard by surprise and in less than one hour came away with a gunboat, two bateaux, anchors, 120 barrels of salt, eight barrels of pork, whiskey and tobacco. No one on either side was hurt.

Fitz had intended a simultaneous raid on Black Rock, an important post opposite Fort Erie down-river from Buffalo. Black Rock would be heavily guarded so he had reserved the rest of his band for this attack. But it proved impossible to get enough boats for his forty men so he had to postpone the raid.

A few days later Lieutenant-Colonel Bisshopp came to Fitz-Gibbon with another plan to attack Black Rock. At this time FitzGibbon had his men hidden in barns near Fort Erie and was busy watching the enemy with a spyglass when Bisshopp and two other redcoats walked up in full view of the enemy, to the great disgust of FitzGibbon. The Americans were not aware that the British had moved so close to the frontier, and he was planning a perfect surprise for them. Bisshopp said he was trying to collect 300 men for the raid, but could only obtain 200. Did Fitz-Gibbon think the place could be taken with so few men? Fitz smiled and said he was ready to take it with forty-four as soon as he had boats. He had already ordered Winder to bring the four bateaux from Chippawa.

Bisshopp laughed, "Oh, then, I need ask you no more questions, but go and bring the two hundred men."

Bisshopp had his men there the following day with enough boats to make the crossing. FitzGibbon would lead the advance and cover the retreat should they be attacked.

"At two the following morning we moved off. My men, being select and good boatmen, soon gained the opposite shore, but, owing to the strength of the current and the boats being filled with men, further down than we intended."

FitzGibbon saw that the boats behind him would be driven even farther down and would be a good half-hour later in landing than his own men. He could see 150 armed enemy militiamen emerging from the barracks to meet them. It looked as if he would have to stage a show and stall for time. There was always a good measure of comedy whenever FitzGibbon was called upon to act, and this scene was no exception. There was mist over the river, and he depended on it to camouflage and, he hoped, magnify the numbers of his men while he advanced ahead of them with his bugler and his flag of truce to meet the American commander, Major Hall.

Mary Agnes FitzGibbon says FitzGibbon met the militiamen with these words: "I see you are all militia, and I do not wish to be killing the husbands, fathers and brothers of your innocent families. You shall all be allowed to retire on parole."

Before he could finish his speech, the militia ranks had broken, and the men were running down the hill to Buffalo as fast as they could go. "Stop your men, Major Hall," he called out, hardly able to keep from laughing, "this is quite irregular while negotiating under a flag of truce."

"I know it, sir," replied the indignant American officer, "but I cannot stop them."

By the time Colonel Bisshopp arrived, FitzGibbon had dismissed Major Hall, who had gone down the hill after his men. The coast was clear for the work to be done. They seized eight large boats into which they put two 12-pounders, one 6-pounder, and a large quantity of military stores and provisions. Half their men were detached to get these stores away. The other half went to work burning the block house, the barracks, which could hold 5,000 men, and a schooner anchored there.

But the party lasted too long. According to Mary Agnes Fitz-Gibbon, her grandfather wanted to get away but Colonel Bisshopp had his eye on 400 barrels of salt down the beach. Meanwhile the burning buildings revealed their numbers to the American militia, now strengthened by a force from Buffalo and a number of Indians. They made a furious attack on the hundred-odd British who remained on shore. Driven to their boats, the British left behind a captain and fifteen men killed or wounded. Another twenty-seven killed or wounded were in their boats. Suddenly someone cried that Colonel Bisshopp was wounded and had been left ashore. A boatload of Green Tigers made a rush for him and got him into their boat where he was wounded twice more. He died five days later from the wounds.

Later FitzGibbon wrote, "For no man fallen in battle, did I grieve so much as for him. He was a man of most gentle and generous nature, and was more beloved by the militia over whom he was an inspecting field officer, than any other who served in the province during the war. But he wanted either experience or judgement, and fell in consequence in the prime of life, in the twenty-eighth year of his age."

Meanwhile, a new commander had arrived to take a larger look at the future of this war. He was Major-General Francis, Baron de Rottenburg. In a letter to Sir George Prevost, written from Twelve Mile Creek, July 7, 1812, he described conditions as he saw them there: "I am using every exertion to repair the roads. They have been much neglected by my predecessor and are the worst I ever saw anywhere." He mentions reinforcing Burlington:

> That stronghold I must retire to ultimately and maintain myself until the navy will be enabled to meet the fleet on Lake Ontario. Had Sir James Yeo time to spare to co-operate with the army, Fort George would have fallen. But I do not now possess means of attacking them on both sides of the river.
>
> Lieut. FitzGibbon is a deserving and enterprising officer and I shall forward your letter to him. [Prevost had apparently written to inform FitzGibbon of his promotion. Mary Agnes FitzGibbon says that letter was lost among Fitz-Gibbon's private papers.]
>
> With the exception of Lieut.-Colonel Harvey, who is a most active, zealous, and intelligent officer, the heads of the departments here are deficient in activity and cleverness, and the militia staff is most miserable. There is a vast deal to be done in this Province. Everything is unhinged and requires my utmost exertions to keep affairs in some shape or other.

It seems de Rottenburg, like Vincent, did not achieve instant understanding with the militia. Merritt gives us a militiaman's reaction to him. "I was presented to Major General de Rottenburg who had arrived to take the command of the army, as well as being President of the Province. He unfortunately brought with him a very great name. We expected he would have performed wonders, in fact he has done nothing but eat, drink, snuff and snuffle."

On July 20 de Rottenburg wrote to Sir George Prevost that he had moved to St. David's, "which reduces the enemy to the ground he stands upon and prevents his getting any supplies from our territory." He also mentioned that it had become necessary to keep the Indians busy, and that they were now busy "harassing and teasing them the whole day long."

The stalemate at Fort George for the rest of the summer was a direct result of the deadlock on Lake Ontario. Earlier in the year Sir James Yeo had had some advantage as Chauncey was staying close to Sackett's Harbour until his new ship *General Pike* would be ready to sail. Yeo had been able to support Vincent's land movement toward Fort George and conduct raids along the south shore of Lake Ontario. But on July 21 the new corvette *General Pike* led Chauncey's squadron out of Sackett's Harbour and Yeo's advantage was lost.

The *General Pike* had twenty-six long 24-pounders and thus would have a greater range of fire than any British ship. Altogether Chauncey had two ships, one brig and ten schooners while Yeo's fleet consisted of two ships, two brigs and two schooners. At Fort Niagara, Chauncey took on troops to attack Vincent's supply depot at Burlington Heights. But this post had been reinforced by Colonel Battersby who had marched from York with part of the Glengarry corps to protect it. Chauncey saw the Glengarries there, realized that York must be defenceless and decided instead to make a second attack on York. On the first of August the Americans landed, burnt barracks and storehouses, and carried away provisions, mainly flour.

On August 7, Sir James Yeo's fleet met Chauncey's off the Niagara River, and a decisive battle seemed inevitable. Instead, the two commanders manoeuvred all night. Around midnight a storm came up and two of Chauncey's schooners capsized and were lost. All but thirteen of the men on board went down with the ships.

Still the two fleets danced around each other for five successive days. In the early hours of August 11, Chauncey's two best schooners became separated from the American fleet and were captured by Yeo. Finally, Chauncey sailed away to Sackett's Harbour with four ships fewer than when he sailed out. Yeo had no desire to tangle with those long guns on the *General Pike*. His only advantage was that he could out-sail the American vessels and occasionally he might cut out one of Chauncey's schooners. The rest of the time he would let Chauncey chase him around Lake Ontario as the two fleets danced a sort of international ballet to the great disgust of land commanders on both sides.

In mid-August excitement stirred the ranks briefly when Sir George Prevost arrived and ordered a "general demonstration" on the morning of August 24. While the larger part of the army performed before Fort George, 350 men under Major Plenderleath crossed the river and used the shelter of the woods to surprise the American soldiers manning the guns and batteries opposite Fort George. Included in this number was FitzGibbon's party of Green Tigers. Fourteen Americans were taken prisoner, the rest driven back to Fort Niagara. Three from the 49th were wounded.

Meanwhile, on the Canadian side of the Niagara, the soldiers were delighted to dash into the town of Fort George. The Americans opened a brisk fire from house windows and garden walls but still the British were "extremely unwilling to come away." Colonel Harvey even stopped at his old quarters to snatch up a box of valuables he had left there. Their pickets all taken prisoner, the main American army stayed inside Fort George. No amount of manoeuvring by Prevost's army could induce them to come out. Prevost's dispatch afterwards said he was convinced that Fort George could not be taken without more troops, help from the fleet, and a battering train.

Prevost said farewell to de Rottenburg and Vincent; he was going back to Kingston to try to convince Sir James Yeo to do something decisive on the water. The troops on the Niagara frontier settled down to being sick.

By the end of August the spirit had gone out of the British on the Niagara frontier. Idleness bred misery as real and awful as the sufferings of battle. Sickness stalked in every camp, and by September 6, de Rottenburg was writing, "I have now in the rear at the Twelve Mile Creek and at York, 500 men sick."

In a private letter to Sir George Prevost August 30, de Rottenburg said, "Colonels Stewart, Plenderleath, May, Williams, FitzGibbon, and a great number of others are laid up with the lake fever. We are in great want of medicine and wine for the sick."

Meanwhile FitzGibbon lay in a fever, possibly cared for by one of his own Green Tigers who had recovered from or not yet caught the fever. He may have remained wherever his band was camped or he may have been conveyed to the crude hospitals set up at the Twelve.

In his September 21 letter home, Ridout mentioned two officers who have died, then adds, "FitzGibbon has got well again."

On September 19 Sir George Prevost wrote to Sir James Lucas Yeo:

> The Centre Division of the Upper Canada Army is placed in a situation very critical and one novel in the system of war, that of investing a force vastly superior in numbers within a strongly entrenched position. It was adopted and has been maintained from a confident expectation that with the squadron under your command a combined attack ere this could have been effected on the enemy at Fort George with every prospect of success. To the local disadvantages of the positions occupied by our army have been added disease and desertion to a degree calling for an immediate remedy.

Inexperienced new troops were arriving from Europe and they had to learn from the militiamen how to make shelters, how to light a smudge against mosquitoes, and how to cook enough to eat. Lieutenant MacEwan of the Royal Scots wrote to his wife, "I now live by myself in an Indian house made of branches and leaves of trees, all that defends me from cold and heat."

But even the militia could not make lean-to shelters to keep out rain; their clothing did not repel water; by this time their boats leaked. More than one regiment was in rags. Merritt's troop had been disbanded because his people were "literally naked and defenceless" and he was sent to Montreal to plead his need for appointments and better organization for his dragoon force.

When it rained on the soldiers their fires went out. What food was available was wet. Rain turned the low ground on which they were camped into swamp. Sanitation was poor in dry weather; in wet, it became a horror and a hazard to health. Dysentery and fever spread misery among the men and so shattered their morale that some no longer dreaded being shot by a Yankee. Others looked across the Niagara and imagined greener fields. Maybe it rained less over there. Everyone imagined more freedom over there, whatever freedom was. Numbers of them deserted to find out. Others tried and failed and were shot. Some sulked and disobeyed and were flogged.

Days dragged on in idleness and lack of purpose while they camped beside an enemy that would not come out to fight. Food grew scarcer. Settlers now hated the sight of redcoats because the soldiers were driven to stealing their apples and potatoes and hay and burned their rail fences for fuel.

Young Thomas Ridout from York had just been appointed to the commissariat at Niagara in July. His letters home show quite plainly how things were. He was posted at St. David's, then moved to the lakeside where 2,000 troops were camped about the beginning of September. A Mr. Thompson had let them into an old unused house on his property.

> We made a straw bed on the floor. We collect balm in the garden for tea, and carry on an extensive robbery of peas, apples, onions, corn, carrots, etc.; for we can get nothing but by stealing, excepting milk, which is carefully measured. Bread and butter is out of the question, and to-day we sent a dragoon to the Twelve-Mile Creek for these articles and G. to the cross-roads for beef, etc. ... The army is getting very sickly, forty or fifty men are sent to hospital every day.
>
> September 16th: We burn rails, steal apples, pears and peaches at a great rate. Old Lion sometimes growls at the

rails going so fast, but can't help himself. He thinks me the most innocent of the lot.

September 21st: We are in the same state at the old house as ever. I carry on the foraging. To-night our dragoon is to make a grand attack upon the onions.

What the British army did not steal, the Indians did. In midsummer General de Rottenburg had found it necessary to issue a District General Order: "The ready sale found for articles by the Indians having encouraged depredations by them, all officers and soldiers are forbidden to purchase anything from an Indian without permission." He announced at the same time that any soldier caught taking hay or burning fences would be tried by "drumhead court martial."

It is too true that our fleet on Lake
Erie is taken, and Procter is left
at Amherstburg without provisions, guns or men. Most of the
cannon were mounted on board
the ships.

Thomas Ridout to his father at
York, September 21, 1813.

10

During that summer of 1813, while Yeo and Chauncey
were playing tag on Lake Ontario, the situation of the British
fleet on Lake Erie under Captain Robert H. Barclay was becoming desperate. The burning of York by the Americans in
April had destroyed the naval stores and guns which were destined for Barclay's brigs under construction at Amherstburg.
Through July his tiny fleet had blockaded the American fleet,
under Captain Perry, in Presqu'Ile harbour where two large
ships were under construction. Barclay knew that a sandbar at
the mouth of the harbour would make it impossible for the
enemy's new ships to sail out unless they removed their cannon.
But on the first of August Barclay sailed to Long Point for provisions and the Americans risked all to get their ships out.
Without cannon they were completely vulnerable to Barclay's
return. The story is told that a public dinner given Barclay by the
citizens of Port Dover kept him away too long. When he got
back Perry's ships had just made their escape.

Now Barclay had to flee to Amherstburg for the rest of the
summer to await the completion of his brig, *Detroit*. By Sep-

tember, Procter's Army of the West was becoming desperate for supplies. The long winter faced Procter with all the western Indians and their families to be fed, and the season for sailing would soon close. Barclay had given up hope of more reinforcements arriving for his fleet. Since he also had no hope of receiving guns for the *Detroit*, he and Procter took guns off the ramparts of Fort Malden for the new ship. Now Barclay, urged by Prevost, decided he would have to go out to confront Perry's fleet.

> That the Risk is very great I feel very much, but that in the present state of this place, without provisions, without stores – and without Indian Goods (which last is a matter of the highest importance), it is necessary, I fully agree with the General. Less can be expected, (if anything at all) than if I had received re-enforcements, which I judge absolutely necessary. *More* I have never asked from you. I am certain of being well supported by the officers, which gives me almost all the confidence I have in the approaching battle."

On Thursday, September 9, Barclay had the weather in his favour. He hoped to use his long guns from Fort Malden against Perry without letting Perry close on him. If he were to close, Perry would be decidedly stronger, with three brigs and six schooners heavily armed with 490 men. Barclay had three brigs and three schooners and 310 seamen. But the wind changed. The British could not keep Perry off. The battle which began just before noon on September 10 and raged for almost four hours inflicted terrible damage. The noise of the cannon were said to be heard at least 160 miles away. And from York, more than 200 miles away, Ridout's diary for that day records that the wind was in the west, the day heavy with rain and loud firing heard toward Niagara about eleven A.M.

The wrecked ships of both squadrons sagged together in the awful quiet after the fight. Sixty-eight men were dead, forty-one British and twenty-seven Americans. Another ninety-four British and ninety-six Americans lay wounded. Captain Barclay himself was badly wounded, with a shattered thigh and a shot in the shoulder of his only arm (he had lost his other arm with Nelson at the Battle of Trafalgar). All his officers were either killed or wounded. The dreadful news did not reach Niagara until September 16. Everyone there knew what it meant: Procter's army at Amherstburg, without provisions for the winter and with the guns of Fort Malden sacrificed on the *Detroit*, would be forced to retreat. The whole upper country would fall. The state of apprehension at the beginning of October is reflected in Thomas Ridout's letters:

> We expect some serious movement every hour, as the enemy are in great force at Fort George. [The enemy fleet was standing by as American troops were loaded into bateaux and there was great fear that they would land above the British and attack.] We are driving all the cattle from this part of the district toward the head of the lake. The Chippawa and Short Hills country is stripped of cattle, and today they have been driving them from the vicinity of the camps. The wagons stand ready loaded with the baggage which moves in the rear. I am sure we shall march soon.

But it was realized before long that the American army was heading east. Between three and four thousand Americans were moving toward Sackett's Harbour, under General Wilkinson; their intention apparently an attack on Kingston. James Fitz-Gibbon soon had orders to march his men to Forty Mile Creek. The 49th Regiment, the 104th, and a corps of Voltigeurs (Provincial Light Infantry from Lower Canada) were being sent to Kingston with all possible speed. On October 4 the men embarked in bateaux and crossed to York and from there they re-embarked October 5 and reached Kingston on October 11. General de Rottenburg was also proceeding swiftly to Kingston. FitzGibbon had gone from Niagara before the next piece of bad news arrived from the west on October 8. Procter's retreating army had moved east along the river Thames followed by the American General Harrison. Here at least they would fight out of reach of American naval power. At the battle of Moraviantown (seventy miles up the Thames River), Procter had made his stand on October 5.

Tecumseh was with Procter although the two men had long ceased to understand each other. Tecumseh failed to see how defeat in a naval battle forced Procter's land force to retreat. For Tecumseh and his people there could be no retreat. In his speech to General Procter on September 18, he expresses the position of his Indian nation with his usual terse eloquence. "Father, you have got the arms and ammunition which our great Father sent to his red children. If you have an idea of going away, give them to us, and you may go, and welcome; our lives are in the hands of the Great Spirit. We are determined to defend our lands and, if it be His will, we wish to leave our bones upon them."

At the battle of Moraviantown, Tecumseh and his Indians fought long after the 41st Regiment had retreated. Tecumseh and his closest leaders never retreated; they all died fighting. The Battle of the Thames took place just one year after Isaac Brock died, and in that year Tecumseh must often have thought of him and longed for his brand of British leadership. Today he died as Brock had died, fighting a desperate fight.

Twenty-eight British officers and 606 men were killed or captured in the fight, 246 British managed to escape. They soon found each other in the woods and managed an orderly retreat to Burlington. Harrison and his American army turned back to Detroit. Meanwhile the sick and sorry army at Niagara had also marched to Burlington. On the fourteenth, Lieutenant-Colonel Glegg wrote, "We arrived here on the twelfth, after undergoing a very harassing march for our poor fellows, particularly the numerous sick, whose pallid countenances cut me to the quick. The elements were most unkind during our retreat but anything was pleasing after quitting that sink of disease on the Twelve Mile Creek, where an inactive residence had nearly annihilated as fine a body of men as were ever led against an enemy."

Thomas Ridout wrote to his father from Burlington, "The times are so gloomy that I know not what to say. We shall soon retreat to Kingston. Every preparation is making. ... We had a most dreadful time from the Crossroads [Homer]. Upwards of three hundred men were straggling upon the road and wagons loaded with miserable objects stuck fast in mud-holes, broken down and unable to ascend the hills, and the men too ill to stir hand or foot. One thousand Western Indians arrived last night from Detroit, besides 2,000 women and children. Poor creatures! What will become of them? It is said the great Tecumseh is killed."

The Governor-in-Chief and Commander of the Forces has the satisfaction to announce to the troops that the corps of observation, with the division of gunboats which he had ordered from Kingston to follow the movements of the enemy's army... has completely defeated a large division of the enemy's army, consisting of cavalry, riflemen and infantry, exceeding four thousand men, which attacked it on the 11th November near Crysler's, about twenty miles above Cornwall, taking from the enemy one field piece and four hundred prisoners.

General Order, Headquarters, La Chine, November 13, 1813.

11

For the men of the 49th, 104th, and the Voltigeurs, not yet stricken by news of Procter's defeat and Tecumseh's death, it was impossible not to enjoy the journey east. As they pushed away from Forty Mile Creek, Fitz felt a new spirit take hold of himself and his men. Nearly all of the men in the boats around him had had to deal with fever, many had lain near death. Muscles were weak now for the long pull on the oars to take them to York. But there was vigour in the very air, and a tang in the October breeze that you could taste, and a sky so solid a blue you felt you could cut it with your sword.

These men were embarking on a race and were keen at the starting line. Along the south shore of Lake Ontario, their Yankee competitors had a head start. The Americans also had an advantage in knowing where they were going. The British leaders all guessed the destination would be Kingston. But speculation went on among the men; some of them bet their boots the Americans intended to attack Montreal. Nobody knew for sure where or when the two racing fleets would meet. Some of the men in the boats would die when they did. In the meantime each man would enjoy the race and be glad he had not died of fever in Niagara.

Their burst of new energy had gone, and they were weary men before they pulled in to York, but a night inside barracks was a rare treat to men accustomed to Indian tepees or barns. In the morning, well fed and rested, they started the long pull for Kingston.

Frost in the air meant the end of disease. Fitz took deep breaths, pure, clean, and cold. He could feel new strength already in his arms. As he looked over his men he felt good about them too; they were all so active and tough by nature that they were regaining power in great style. In some of the other boats the men were not so well and would be hard put to pull themselves from York to Kingston.

Apart from the vagaries of war, FitzGibbon had another reason to be glad that he was moving east. He loved a girl named Mary Haley, and it was almost a year now since he had seen her. She was the daughter of George Haley who had come from England to fight in the American Revolution as a British soldier under Burgoyne. After the close of the Revolution he had settled on a grant of land in Leeds County.

The war had kept James and Mary apart but she was always there in the back of his mind and whenever he had a moment free from the work of war it was to Mary his thoughts would run. Sometimes now it was hard to picture her face exactly but her presence was always there, the warmth and joy, her unique importance to him. If he had a life to live after this war he wanted to live it with Mary.

On October 11, Major-General Darroch was writing from Kingston: "The 104th, 49th, and Voltigeurs are arrived but do not look over well. I hope the troops with the Centre Division are in better health than these seem to be."

As it turned out Fitz and the rest of the advance troops had almost a month in Kingston. Mary may have travelled there to see him. It is unlikely that he could go farther east to her home as he and the rest of the 49th were part of a "corps of observation" which would be sent in pursuit whenever the Americans made a move out of Sackett's Harbour. But if the British assumed the Americans knew where they were going, they were wrong. Back in August, John Armstrong, the Secretary of War, had spelled out the need to either attack and capture Kingston or go down the St. Lawrence and cut off communication above Cornwall (roughly where Morrisburg now stands). Major-General Wilkinson, who had command of the American army from Lake Champlain to the Niagara frontier, had hurried up to Niagara but immediately got the fever. So there he stayed until October 2 when the British witnessed his departure with Chauncey's fleet and 6,000 troops. The voyage to Sackett's Harbour was not easy, as the Americans got caught in severe storms and squalls. News carried by a spy to Kingston in mid-October said that a number of boats and a number of men had been lost on Sandy Beach. The British spy also reported that Wilkinson had intended to attack Kingston but on hearing that the British fleet had arrived there with reinforcements ahead of him, had changed his mind.

On October 17, Wilkinson moved his troops to Grenadier Island eighteen miles from Kingston, poised either for an attack on that town or for a run down the St. Lawrence. Meanwhile he was writing to the Secretary of War and to Major General Wade Hampton, in command of the Lake Champlain army, proposing an attack on Montreal and telling Hampton when and where to meet him. Wade Hampton happened to have an intense personal dislike for Wilkinson and was not inclined to take orders from him. By October 19, the Secretary of War was writing to Wilkinson like this:

> [Kingston] would probably surround us with all the embarrassments of a Canadian winter and extinguish every hope of grasping the other, the safer and the greater object below. I call it the safer and the greater object because ... at Montreal you find the weaker place and the smaller force to encounter; at Montreal you meet a fresh, unexhausted efficient reinforcement of four thousand men.

Meanwhile the hapless men of the American army waited on Grenadier Island, victims of the indecision of their superiors and an overdose of rain, wind, and snow. As an officer wrote on October 26,

Here we are at the east end of Lake Ontario, pelted daily with the inexhaustible rains, which seem to be collected and poured upon us from all lakes and swamps between this and Lake Superior. We have indeed for nearly a month been exposed to such torrents as you have no idea of in your part of the world. In consequence of the bad weather our troops from Fort George and Sackett's Harbour have been scattered everywhere along the coast, many having staved their boats, but most of them have now arrived here.

And on November 1, Wilkinson wrote, "The wind and waves and rains and snow still prevail, and we have made several fruitless attempts to turn Stony Point, one of them at great peril to three thousand men, whom I seasonably remanded to the harbour without the loss of a life."

The weather was falling on Canadians as well, as Thomas Ridout could testify. While FitzGibbon and most of the troops had moved east by water, Ridout and the Commissariat Department were travelling by land. They had left Burlington on the eighteenth and Thomas had a day at home in York before they pushed on. It took an incredible ten days to get from York to Kingston. On November 1, he wrote of the miserable journey they had had:

We have had a most harassing journey of ten days to this place, where we arrived last night in a snow-storm. It has been snowing all day, and is now half a foot deep. The journey has knocked Mr. Couche up. He is in the next room with a fever. Frequently I had to go middle deep in a mudhole, unload the wagon, and carry heavy trunks fifty yards, sometimes waist-deep in mire, and reload the wagon. One night it upset going up a steep hill in the woods. Gee and I carried the load up to the top, whilst Mr. C. rode on three miles in the rain for a lanthorn. About eleven o'clock we got in, when we missed a trunk with 500 guineas in it. Mr. Couche and I immediately rode back about two miles and found it in a mudhole. ...

Accounts have just arrived from Montreal saying that four hundred of our troops have defeated General Hampton's army of four thousand men.

The battle Ridout referred to would be known as the Battle of Châteauguay (October 25-26) and would become a proud piece of Canadian history. The American Secretary of War had ordered Hampton to move with 4,000 men from New York State up the Châteauguay River to where it empties into the St. Lawrence close to Montreal and there "hold the enemy in check," while awaiting Wilkinson.

Meanwhile Lieutenant-Colonel de Salaberry led his own Voltigeurs, several militia companies, and some Indians a few miles up the Châteauguay where he prepared a defensive reception for the Americans. Hampton sent 1,500 Americans under Colonel Purdy on a circuitous fifteen-mile trail through the woods to outflank de Salaberry's men. They got thoroughly lost. In the morning Hampton's main body attacked de Salaberry's advance picket of 300 militia and a few Indians on the left bank, while Purdy's detachment finally found and attacked the 160 militiamen on the other side of the river.

Behind de Salaberry, the Canadian rear guard was led by Lieutenant-Colonel "Red" George Macdonell with 1,130 men, and they now set up a tremendous racket in the woods to unnerve the Americans. Hampton began to withdraw his army up the Châteauguay and back over the border into New York State.

The Battle of Châteauguay was fought without the British army. All the defenders were Canadian. Their successful rout of the Americans sent a wave of pride up the St. Lawrence and young Canadians like Ridout were eager to get on with the awful journey east.

FitzGibbon and the rest of the British also took new heart. They had embarked at Niagara with the defeat on Lake Erie ringing in their ears. Hard on their heels had followed the news of Procter's defeat in the west. This victory in the east was like a dose of good medicine that they all needed badly. If they were to meet the entire American army at Montreal, it was good to know de Salaberry and his men would be there too.

It was becoming evident that they *would* meet at Montreal. By

November 5 Wilkinson's entire army was on the move through the Thousand Islands: four regiments of infantry, two regiments of dragoons, and three regiments of artillery. Chauncey had moved his fleet into the river to protect the departure of the troops. He would stay there until the army could pass below Prescott, then "use every exertion to get out of the river as soon as possible." By November 6, Wilkinson wrote to Hampton, "I am destined to and determined on the attack of Montreal if not prevented by some act of God, and to give security to the enterprise, the division under your command must co-operate with the corps under my immediate orders." That same day, de Rottenburg released his "corps of observation" after the Americans.

FitzGibbon says they left about ten o'clock at night, under the command of Lieutenant-Colonel Joseph W. Morrison of the 89th. FitzGibbon's own regiment was "reduced by the previous campaigns to little more than 200 strong." The 89th amounted to 450 men. They had a few artillerymen and two 6-pounder field guns. They travelled in two schooners under the command of Captain Mulcaster (Yeo's favourite officer) along with seven gunboats and a number of bateaux. Mulcaster's armed schooners could go no further than Prescott but his gunboats would take care of any American boats that lagged behind down river.

The St. Lawrence has never seen, before or since, such a sight as the movement of the American army of eight to ten thousand men down to Montreal. Three hundred bateaux swept along, as well as a variety of other small boats, followed by twelve gunboats to protect their rear. Thomas Ridout, as he travelled the Canadian shore, recorded the colour and commotion, the splendid pageantry, and the shock wave of alarm as they moved along. From Prescott he wrote:

> It was a grand sight to see any army of 10,000 men going down the Gallette rapids. They fired at us several shots, taking our wagon for artillery, I suppose. Every boat had a gun mounted, and carried about sixty men. About 180 immense boats went down full of men, besides schooners with provisions. ... The Americans seem confident of taking Montreal. I never witnessed such a beautiful sight as the army going down the rapids.

While Ridout stopped at Prescott, Morrison's corps of observation had arrived and collected a detachment of 240 troops commanded by Lieutenant-Colonel Pearson consisting of two flank companies of the 49th, some Canadian Fencibles, three companies of Voltigeurs and a few militia artillerymen with a 6-pounder gun as well as a few dragoons to carry messages. Ridout wrote, "Yesterday Colonels Harvey and Pearson left us with 1,500 regulars and eight gunboats in pursuit, determined to attack the enemy wherever they are to be found."

Actually Morrison's force now amounted to 900 men although Ridout guessed at 1,500. The British must have looked like a tiny fish determined to bite the tail of a whale.

On November 6, Wilkinson stopped seven miles above Ogdensburg in order to "pass Prescott this night after the setting of the moon." He landed his men above Ogdensburg and sent each bateau down with a picked crew while gunboats guarded their front and their left flanks against exposure to the guns of Prescott's Fort Wellington. Most of the troops – and the powder and ammunition – moved by land past the British batteries to re-embark below Ogdensburg. Below Prescott every farmer seemed to be down on the shore taking shots at the Americans floating past. When Wilkinson had had enough of this sport, he ordered 1,200 troops to land at Point Iroquois and drive them off. This formidable array of Americans nearly captured young Ridout. In his letter from Prescott he tells what happened:

> Yesterday we got thirteen miles below this and were obliged to return on account of the landing of the American army half a mile below us on our side. We had the most narrow escape of being taken. Mr. Green only rode on a few hundred yards farther, and was taken prisoner. ...
>
> [Later.] Good fortune attends me, for there never was a more narrow escape than when the Yankees landed twelve miles below Prescott. We slept within 200 yards of them. Mr. Green was taken prisoner three minutes after he had left us. Next morning they departed, and Mr. Couche sent me down to reconnoitre and inquire for him. I rode down two and a half miles, but the whole river above and below

was covered with their boats; some pulled toward the shore where I was, and came within fifty yards, when a man came running to me and told me by all means to make my escape, for that six boats had landed above me. I instantly galloped back, and passed before they reached the road, as they had landed on a small wooded point 300 yards away. The man told me afterwards that I had hardly got out of sight, when they took three prisoners.

After this Ridout and his party kept behind the "corps of observation," and Colonel Harvey, who was moving part of the corps east by land, "promised to clear the road."

From the second of November until the tenth, the weather had been clear, dry and mild. But on the night of November 10, cold sleet fell, showing no favour to either army. In the vicinity of present-day Morrisburg, British and Canadian and American soldiers crawled under their boats or huddled beneath lean-to shelters or, if very lucky, found a friendly barn. At least Lieutenant-Colonel Morrison was snug and dry; he had established headquarters in John Crysler's big farmhouse. He liked the look of the terrain here as well as any for meeting the Americans.

The Americans had stopped just below Crysler's at the head of the Long Sault Rapids. Wilkinson had suffered an attack of fever again and had been unwell for the whole distance down the St. Lawrence. Now he sent Brigadier-General Jacob Brown ashore with 2,500 men to clear the way to Cornwall. Meanwhile Brigadier-General John Parke Boyd was to take the troops which could be spared from getting boats through the Long Sault Rapids, and turn back on the British force.

The rain had stopped by Thursday morning, November 11. The morning was bleak and cold and grey when Boyd's 2,000 regulars advanced on John Crysler's farm. A road ran north from the farmhouse and along it the 49th and six companies of the 89th were positioned facing east with log fences for cover. They looked toward a field of fall wheat and beyond it to where the King's Road crossed two gullies and a large ravine. Between the two gullies and stretching to the river, Morrison had placed Pearson's detachment from Prescott. Three companies of the 89th with three 6-pounder guns, protected Pearson's men on the inland side. Three companies of Voltigeurs were placed in the large ravine as skirmishers and about thirty Indians waited in the woods.

The Americans soon got past the grey-clad Voltigeurs but at about two o'clock they were stopped by the 49th and 89th. Fitz-Gibbon, in a letter written years later, said:

> The 49th wore their gray great-coats, while the 89th appeared in their scarlet uniform. General Covington, supposing the men in gray to be Canadian militia, called aloud to his men saying, "Come lads, let me see how you will deal with these militia men," but on their advancing the 49th, who as yet were calmly standing in open column under the fire of the enemy's skirmishers, quickly wheeled into line and commenced firing regularly by platoons which soon threw the advancing Americans into confusion and drove them back beyond the range of fire.

The Americans then tried to get around the British on their left, but Morrison wheeled the 89th around to stop them. Now Captain Mulcaster's guns were attacking Wilkinson's headquarters boat.

FitzGibbon finishes the story: "General Covington being killed, the Americans soon after retreated to their own shore and ultimately went into winter quarters, abandoning altogether their intended attack upon Montreal."

The final blow to Wilkinson was a letter received the next morning from Hampton, who refused to meet him at St. Regis. Wilkinson, tired and sick on that grey November morning on the St. Lawrence, was facing his own failure. There would be no attack on Montreal.

> From the St. Lawrence to the ocean an open disregard prevails for the laws prohibiting inter-course with the enemy. The road to St. Regis is covered with droves of cattle and the river with rafts destined for the enemy. The revenue officers see these things but acknowledge their inability to put a stop to such outrageous proceedings. On the eastern side of Lake Champlain the high roads are found insufficient for the supplies of cattle which are pouring into Canada. Like herds of buffaloes, they press through the forest making paths for themselves.
>
> Major-General Izard to the Secretary of War, camped near Plattsburg, July 31, 1814.

12

FitzGibbon spent Christmas of 1813 in Montreal, while the disheartened Americans camped in winter quarters on the Salmon River south and east of Cornwall. The celebrations were gay in Montreal that year with so many redcoats in town. To the soldier it was almost unreal to dance at a ball and sleep in a bed and eat Christmas goose after the privations and sufferings of the year past.

Because they knew what 1814 would bring, the soldiers' enjoyment of these brief good times was even keener. News recently in from the Niagara frontier had changed the tone of this war and it would no longer be considered a "nice" war involving only professional soldiers and volunteer militiamen. When the Americans left the Niagara frontier to sweep down to Montreal, Brigadier-General George McClure remained with a handful of troops to guard Fort George. When two new British commanders, Lieutenant-General Gordon Drummond and Major-General Phineas Riall, arrived in Upper Canada, McClure guessed that he was no longer safe in Fort George. On December 10, a cold, damp, winter day, he decided to withdraw across the Niagara. Before going he turned out into the snow 450 women and children, and burned the town of Newark. The inhabitants had exactly half an hour to carry away something for their survival.

When General Drummond with Colonel Murray of the 100th Regiment arrived, the town was still smoking. The two leaders lost little time deciding to retaliate.

On December 19, Colonel Murray took the flank companies of the 41st and 100th, some militia, artillery, and the Grenadier company of the 1st Royals across the Niagara River. The fight was short and soon a British flag flew over Fort Niagara. Murray was delighted to seize a large quantity of clothing and tents and general camp equipage which would help the suffering townspeople at Newark.

A cannon, fired from Fort Niagara, was a signal of Murray's success to General Riall who waited at Queenston. Riall's troops then crossed the Niagara and destroyed Lewiston. It was to be a black Christmas for Americans living on the Niagara frontier, caught in a relentless wave of British vengeance. A few nights after Lewiston burned, troops again crossed the Niagara to burn Youngstown, Tuscarora Village, Fort Schlosser, Black Rock, and Buffalo. A letter from a gentleman at Canandaigua, published in the *National Advocate*, New York, December 31, portrays the full horror of the time:

> The Indians and British are in the full tide of successful retaliation: 300 families (says Captain Parish, Indian agent) are now on their way to this place, and the most miserable sufferers, and many children without either stockings or shoes. All here is alarm and commotion. *O horrida bella! Horrida bella!* Porter's mills at Schlosser are burnt. Two sons of Benjamin Barton, Esq., are killed.

Meanwhile in Montreal, the end of 1813 was, for FitzGibbon, the end of his association with the 49th. Actually there was little left of the 49th. From a regiment of ten companies which Brock had proudly called one of the best in 1812, the 49th had been reduced by the ravages of war to 160 men for the Battle of Crysler's Farm. At that battle, Thomas Ridout says in a letter home, the 49th lost sixty more men, killed and wounded. Each of the 49th left alive to celebrate that Christmas of 1813 in Montreal must have considered his hold on life a kind of miracle.

When the January thaw was over and movement easy again on the ice, the St. Lawrence came alive with the goings and comings of the army. By far the strangest activity was the crossing of sleighloads of flour and droves of cows from the American side of the river to the Canadian. The Americans along the lower St. Lawrence and in all the northeastern states had not been able to work up a pure hatred for their Canadian neighbours. Most of them had been opposed to this war in the first place, and apart from any ties of the heart, they were Yankees and not prone to pass up an opportunity to make a dollar. As the war went on and the British became short of supplies, the opportunities for making money got better and better. Thomas Ridout who had been appointed Deputy Assistant-Commissary-General and was moving to Cornwall to supply that post, describes how the strange business was carried on:

> There are 1,600 troops there to be fed, and my duty will be hard, for the country is so excessively poor that our supplies are all drawn from the American side of the river. They drive droves of cattle from the interior under pretence of supplying the army at Salmon River, and are so allowed to pass the guards, and at night cross them over to our side. I shall also be under the necessity of getting most of my flour from their side.

In mid-January FitzGibbon moved upriver to Kingston to join his new regiment, the Glengarry Light Infantry Fencibles. At the beginning of February, Wilkinson's army moved from Salmon River; 2,000 of his men went west to Sackett's Harbour under Brigadier-General Brown and the remainder of his army withdrew to Plattsburgh. During the rest of February, raiding parties scooted across the frozen river to plunder sleighloads of provisions from Salmon River, Malone, and the Four Corners. Some of it was plunder which the Americans had taken from Canadian merchants the previous fall.

On March 30, Wilkinson made a half-hearted attack on the British post at Lacolle River, then withdrew from military life. His army had retired to Plattsburgh, and on May 1, thirty-seven-year-old Major-General George Izard took over the command there.

Early in March, Quebec City cheered in the 2nd Battalion of the 8th Regiment and a detachment of the Royal Navy and Royal Marines who had travelled overland from New Brunswick. (A year before the 104th Regiment had made the same epic journey in colder, harsher weather.) The men of the Royal Navy and Royal Marines were bound for Yeo's ships and continued on foot from Quebec to Kingston. When they reached that place at the end of March, they had been fifty-three days on the road.

FitzGibbon's winter in Kingston had been pleasant enough. He had time to drill his men to the high standards of fitness he demanded. The Glengarries were an excellent regiment, as he knew already from their record in battle. Previously Fitz had worked with men who were Irish or British; these men were all Canadian-born, mostly Catholic Scots from Glengarry County, east of Cornwall. His association with them would help to make him Canadian, too. Mary Haley was another influence making him Canadian. From Kingston he often had time to travel east to Leeds County where the Haleys lived, and spend a day with Mary and her family. Mary had knitted him enough socks to last out the coming campaign if he never stopped marching. She had heard too many stories of soldiers going barefoot on the Niagara frontier; she could not make shoes but at least she could supply socks.

FitzGibbon and Mary knew they were in love with each other and may have begun to talk of marriage. But once navigation opened on the lakes, Fitz had other things to think about. On April 14 he watched Yeo launch two new ships, the H.M.S. *Prince Regent* and the H.M.S. *Princess Charlotte*, which would give the British at least temporary superiority over Chauncey. The ships were ready to sail on May 3, and Yeo and Drummond decided on an immediate attack on Oswego, near Sackett's Harbour, to capture guns and naval stores and army provisions. Drummond had wanted to attack Sackett's Harbour itself but Prevost would not spare him enough troops from Lower Canada. He wrote to Drummond that the views of His Majesty's Government "do not justify my exposing too much on one shake. It is by wary measures and occasional daring enterprises with apparently disproportionate means, that the character of the war has been sustained, and from that policy I am not disposed to depart."

As well as six companies of De Watteville's Regiment and the light company of the Glengarry Infantry Fencibles, Yeo had the 2nd Batallion of Royal Marines and detachments of Royal Artillery, Royal Sappers and Miners and Royal Marine Artillery. They landed at Oswego, in the morning, on May 6, and climbed a long steep hill in the face of enemy fire, the Glengarries on the left flank. The American commander fell back from the fort, and the attackers moved in to seize flour, pork, salt, seven long guns, and ordnance stores. The British loss was eighteen killed and seventy-three wounded. But the guns for Chauncey's new ships, the U.S.S. *Superior*, and a brig under construction, were not found. When Yeo soon discovered that they were still at Oswego Falls, he sailed off to blockade that place. On the night of May 28, one of Chauncey's commanders attempted to get away with nineteen bateaux carrying twenty-one long 32-pounder guns, thirteen smaller guns, and ten heavy cables. The British captured one bateau and then tracked down the other eighteen which were pulled into Sandy Creek, just eight miles from Sackett's Harbour, awaiting a further escort.

One of Yeo's commanders, Stephen Popham, with three gunboats, four smaller craft, and 200 sailors and marines, went up Sandy Creek to attack them with no idea that 130 American riflemen and 120 Oneida Indians lay in ambush for them. The British were literally "caught up a creek." After losing fourteen killed and twenty-eight wounded, Popham surrendered his 200 men prisoners to the Americans.

The guns for the U.S.S. *Superior* reached Chauncey while Yeo, down-in-the-mouth, sailed back to Kingston. Chauncey's 62-gun ship would give the Americans command of Lake Ontario. Yeo would have to play the cautious part again until his own 112-gun ship, *St. Lawrence*, could be completed.

On April 14, Sir George Prevost, in Montreal, received good

news from Lord Bathurst in London. A defeated Napoleon was banished to the Isle of Elba. This would mean that troops from Wellington's army would be available to fight in the Canadas. By June 3 he was writing that the 4th Battalion of the Royal Scots, the Nova Scotia Fencibles and troops from the 6th and 82nd Regiments were already on their way, amounting to 3,127 rank and file. Another 10,000 would be dispatched to the Canadas within the course of the year.

The Americans, of course, also got news of the British reinforcements and knew how little time they had. After disagreeing again during the winter months whether to attack Kingston in the spring (Secretary of War Armstrong had hoped Prevost would send troops to Lake Erie and thus weaken Kingston which he could then take "by a *coup de main*"), it was decided in mid-March to fight again on the Niagara Peninsula. Here at least the Americans had behind them an American-held Lake Erie. With Fort Niagara in British hands they would use the Buffalo – Fort Erie entrance to Canada and then move on Fort George.

Now for the first time in this war, the Americans were bringing top-notch commanders and well-trained troops against the British. Major-General Brown from Sackett's Harbour had come up from the New York militia to be one of the best American generals. With him at Niagara was Brigadier-General Winfield Scott from Virginia who was proving himself an able leader in the campaigns of this war. When news of Napoleon's defeat reached America, these two men knew what they had to do. Brown's army crossed the Niagara above Niagara Falls early on July 3. Scott's troops crossed below Fort Erie, while another brigade under Brigadier-General Eleazer Ripley landed above. The two British companies that guarded Fort Erie soon surrendered.

As soon as the news reached Fort George, Major-General Riall reinforced the garrison at Chippawa four miles above Niagara Falls. He was not aware, however, of the fall of Fort Erie, nor did he realize how superbly trained were these American soldiers until he took his 1,500 regulars, 300 militia and Indians against Scott's advancing army on July 5. Although British and Americans were almost equal in numbers in this Battle of Chippawa, the British suffered severely, losing 148 dead compared to forty-eight Americans. Riall managed to get his troops back across the Chippawa, and two days later, when the Americans crossed upstream on the Chippawa, he fell back all the way to Fort George.

FitzGibbon and the Glengarries were still at York playing a waiting game. They were to remain at York until the 89th Regiment reached that place. Meanwhile the 6th, 82nd, and 90th Regiments, sailing from Europe, were nearing Montreal but it would take considerable time to get them up to Niagara. The situation was desperate now. Orders were quickly changed: "The Glengarry Light Infantry to be pushed on to Burlington without waiting for the arrival of the 89th Regiment, leaving all non-effectives at York."

Meanwhile Riall had left sparse garrisons at Fort George, at Fort Missassauga (built on Missassauga Point from the bricks and rubble of the burned town of Newark), and at Fort Niagara, and had moved toward Burlington with close to 900 men. The 103rd Regiment from Burlington under Colonel Hercules Scott was moving forward to meet Riall at Twenty Mile Creek. Together they would attempt to attack the enemy's rear by the Short Hills and Lundy's Lane. The 103rd were at Twenty Mile Creek by July 15. Not far behind them was the Glengarry Regiment marching from York.

Drummond wrote to Sir George Prevost from Kingston on July 13: "The enemy have established themselves at Queenston, where they have placed guns on Mr. Hamilton's house and commenced fortifying the heights." Drummond travelled with the 89th Regiment and reached York on July 22. From there, he wrote of the desperate situation. Getting men up to Niagara fast enough was one thing; finding provisions to feed them would be another. Two brigs had reached York safely, loaded with provisions, and two brigades of bateaux were on their way, "Which if they arrive in safety will further relieve us, tho' even then our supply will be very far from sufficient. I have therefore been under the necessity of ordering all the women and children, of the Troops, to be sent down from Niagara, Burlington, and

York, and the families of the Indians to be placed on Half Allowance, with a view of decreasing as much as possible the issues." It was also becoming impracticable to keep the militia called out because this was harvest time and "the whole produce of the neighbouring country is in the greatest danger of being lost."

While Drummond was worrying and hurrying to Niagara, General Jacob Brown, sitting with his Americans on Queenston Heights, was equally uncomfortable. Brown had counted on the cooperation of Chauncey's fleet to take Fort George but each day as he looked vainly toward Lake Ontario, his desperation rose. Finally on July 13 he wrote to Chauncey:

> I have looked for your fleet with the greatest anxiety since the 10th. I do not doubt my ability to meet the enemy in the field, and to march in any direction over his country – your fleet carrying for me the necessary supplies. We can threaten Forts George and Niagara, and carry that place. For God's sake let me see you. Sir James will not fight; two of his vessels are now in the Niagara.
>
> If you conclude to meet me at the head of the lake and that immediately, have the goodness to bring the guns and troops that I have ordered from the harbour; at all events have the politeness to let me know what aid I am to expect from the fleet of Lake Ontario.

His 2,600 troops, now pressed close against Fort George, were in an extremely vulnerable position, unable to get supplies easily and with no reinforcements available, and harassed continually by the Canadians. Major McFarland of the 23rd U.S. Infantry wrote to his wife, "The whole population is against us; not a foraging party but is fired on, and not unfrequently returns with missing numbers." Finally on July 19, the Americans burned every house between the Falls and Queenston, including the village of St. David's. McFarland wrote:

> This was done within three miles of our camp, and my battalion was sent to cover the retreat, as they had been sent to scour the country and it was presumed they might be pursued. My God, what a service! I never witnessed such a

scene, and had not the commanding officer of the party, Lieut.-Colonel Stone, been disgraced and sent out of the army, I would have resigned.

By July 22, Riall had moved his forces up to Twelve Mile Creek. That day he sent Captain FitzGibbon forward with a party to reconnoitre and gain information of the enemy's intention. It was an old game to FitzGibbon, and played on familiar ground.

Fitz took his party up the heights of Queenston without being seen by an American. What he saw below him was the entire American army strung out in a column on the River Road, stretching from DePuisaye's House, near Newark, almost to Queenston. The wagons and baggage seemed to be halted at Brown's Point. The column began moving towards St. David's, and when about a thousand men joined the march in that direction, it was again halted. From all appearances the American army was falling back on Queenston. FitzGibbon had to leave the hill quite suddenly as a body of cavalry and riflemen advanced on him. He and his party escaped through St. David's, pursued by Americans about a mile beyond that place. As Fitz pounded on through the heat of the July afternoon toward Twelve Mile Creek, he and his men were silent; the oppressive sight of that well-ordered blue army on Canadian soil set heavy in their heads. Each of them knew that hard fighting lay immediately ahead, the Americans desperate and determined to take this frontier before Wellington's troops could reach it.

Fitz was thinking that this summer of 1814 would be different from the days in 1813 when he and his Green Tigers had made the war a game and tailored it to their own talents. Grinning, Fitz remembered a day when he had doubled over with laughter inside a cave while the blue-coats above him were running in terror from his echo.

The grin faded. For the first time ever, James FitzGibbon was seriously considering the possibility of being killed. He wished he had married Mary Haley before he left Kingston. He was a captain now. If he died, she, as his wife, would receive the pension of a captain's widow. That much at least he could have left her. But how in the world could he marry her now?

He shook the thought of Mary out of his head and yelled at his men to ride harder. By three o'clock he had delivered his report of the American movement to Riall at Twelve Mile Creek. Riall, who had already written to Drummond once today, hastened another letter off to him.

On the evening of the 25th instant, at the Falls of Niagara, we
met the enemy and had, I believe,
one of the most desperately
fought actions ever experienced
in America.

13

Colonel James Miller, Fort Erie,
July 28, 1814.

The Battle of Lundy's Lane was fought within a mile of the Falls of Niagara. The roar of the great waterfall formed a background to the terrible noise and confusion of that desperate battle. Today the site is known as Drummond Hill Cemetery, and in it Americans, Canadians, and British lie buried together.

The movement FitzGibbon saw beginning on July 22 continued until Brown had reached Chippawa on the twenty-fourth. Here he received fresh supplies from Fort Schlosser and started a cross-country march on Burlington. On Monday morning, July 25, Riall threw out the Glengarries and the Incorporated Militia (1,000 in all under Lieutenant-Colonel Pearson) as an advance guard to watch the enemy. They took up a position on a hill where Lundy's Lane crossed the Portage, or River, Road. Just at this time Lieutenant-General Drummond reached Fort George with the 89th Regiment and took over command. On the American side of the river he ordered 500 troops and Indians under Lieutenant-Colonel Tucker to move out from Fort Niagara to attack Lewiston. On the Canadian side he sent Colonel Morrison with the 89th to join Riall's 1,500 men already marching to join Pearson's advance at Lundy's Lane.

Actually the attack on Lewiston had been called off because the enemy troops had moved out of Lewiston before Tucker's troops could get underway. Tucker's troops now crossed the river at Queenston where they met Morrison and Drummond on their way to Niagara Falls and Lundy's Lane. Part of the 500 joined Morrison's march; the rest were sent to defend Fort George.

When the Americans attacked about six P.M. on July 25, Drummond had 1,600 men in line on the north slope of the hill, with two 24-pounder guns at the top. The Glengarry Regiment was positioned on the right. What followed was the fiercest, roughest, wildest fight in the war. British artillerymen were bayoneted in the act of loading their guns. Soon American guns were blasting within a few yards of British guns, while infantrymen were fighting hand to hand for control of guns and hill. As darkness fell the confusion increased. Major-General Riall, badly wounded, was unfortunately carried by his stretcher-bearers smack into a party of American cavalry who took him prisoner. On the hilltop it sometimes became impossible to tell which guns were whose; at one point the British loaded an American gun on their limber (front of a gun carriage) while the Americans limbered up a British gun, the two armies thus making a trade.

About nine o'clock the firing stopped briefly. Brigadier-General Winfield Scott was down to 600 effective men, and Brown ordered the brigades of Ripley and Porter brought up to resume the fighting. The exhausted British began falling back until Colonel Hercules Scott's 103rd Regiment marched in from Burlington with 1,200 men. British and Americans fought in the darkness within paces of one another until almost midnight. Finally with 171 Americans killed, 84 British killed and more than 1,110 men wounded altogether, the firing ceased. The two American generals, Brown and Scott, were both severely wounded, and Brigadier-General Ripley withdrew his exhausted and extremely thirsty men back to Chippawa.

An American doctor described the terrible scene on the hill

the next day: "The dead had not been removed during the night, and such a scene of carnage I never beheld, particularly at Lundy's Lane, red coats and blue and grey were promiscuously intermingled, in many places three deep, and around the hill where the enemy's artillery was carried by Colonel Miller, the carcasses of 60 and 70 horses disfigured the scene."

The next morning saw the Americans throwing their heavy baggage into the rapids above Niagara Falls, destroying the bridge at Chippawa, and falling back to Fort Erie.

General Drummond, suffering from a painful neck wound, was slow in following the Americans to Fort Erie. Had he moved faster he might have attacked a weak, unfinished fort but the Americans worked day and night to build rear bastions and complete a deep ditch with seven-foot earthworks and a half mile of trenches and parapet breastworks along the shore. Near the shore a new stonework was built which would be known as the Douglas battery, and on a sand mound called Snake Hill a new bastion, twenty feet high, would bristle with five guns.

FitzGibbon had come through the Battle of Lundy's Lane unscathed. In Drummond's report of the battle, he said, "The Glengarry Light Infantry, under Lieutenant-Colonel Battersby, displayed most valuable qualities as light troops." Now as Drummond moved forward, reaching the heights opposite Black Rock on August 2, he sent the Glengarries ahead driving in the American pickets. On August 4 he wrote of sending "a party of dragoons and a few mounted men of the Glengarry Light Infantry by the road leading upon Fort Erie by Bird's and Tyce Horn's, along the lake shore, to make an accurate reconnoissance of the enemy's position."

The British camp was set up in the woods about two miles from Fort Erie. Now, as American soldiers worked through the hot August days to make Fort Erie a strong fortification, British troops sweated to build a line of batteries about 600 yards from Fort Erie from which to batter it down. While this building went on, FitzGibbon and his men were continually involved in skirmishes that recalled the Green Tiger days of last summer. American riflemen would attack their advance pickets and try to dislodge them or to spy out what the British intended to do next. Drummond wrote to Sir George Prevost:

> These attacks tho' feeble and invariably repulsed, yet harass our troops and occasion us some loss. ... I cannot forbear of taking this occasion of expressing to Your Excellency my most marked approbation of the uniform exemplary good conduct of the Glengarry Light Infantry and Incorporated Militia, the former under command of Lieutenant-Colonel Battersby, and the latter under Major Kerby. ... These two corps have constantly been in close contact with the enemy's outposts and riflemen during the severe service of the last fortnight; their steadiness and gallantry as well as their superiority as light troops have on every occasion been conspicuous.

Dr. William Dunlop ("Tiger" Dunlop) came to Canada in 1814 as an army surgeon and arrived just in time to deal with the appalling number of wounded from Lundy's Lane. But when those men had either died or recovered, Dunlop became bored with his inactive life and transferred to the combat field before Fort Erie. Here he was in close contact with the Glengarries and their methods of bush warfare. He wrote of his admiration for this method of fighting:

> There a man ceases to be merely a part of a machine, or a point in a long line. Both his personal safety and his efficiency depend on his own knowledge and tact. ...
>
> Perhaps there can be no military scene more fit for the pencil than a body of light infantry awaiting an attack. The variety of attitudes necessary to obtain cover— the breathless silence — the men attentive by eye and ear—every glance (furtively lowered) directed to the point—some kneeling, some lying down, and some standing straight behind a tree — the officer with his silver whistle in his hand, ready to give the signal to commence firing, and the bugle boy looking earnestly in his officer's face waiting for the next order. ...
>
> The Glengarry Regiment, being provincials, possessed

many excellent shots. They were not armed with the rifle, but with what I greatly prefer to that arm, the double sighted light infantry musket. ...

During the whole time we lay before Fort Erie, bush-skirmishing was an every day's occurrence, and though the numbers lost in each of these affairs may seem but trifling, yet the aggregate of men put *hors de combat* in a force so small as ours became very serious in the long run.

Dunlop tells a story of getting lost with FitzGibbon:

One day, when relieved from picket, I announced to Col. P., who commanded our brigade, that I had discovered a short way through the woods to the camp, and accordingly I led the way, he and Captain F., of the Glengarries, following. By some fatality I mistook the path, and took a wrong turn, so that instead of finding the camp we came right on the top of an American picket, which opened fire upon us at about fifty yards distance. Being used to this we were behind trees in a moment, and the next were scampering in different directions at greater or less angles from the enemy.

In the midst of the siege of Fort Erie, on August 14, 1814, the Green Tiger astounded his friends by going off to Adolphustown, near Kingston, to get married. It is even more remarkable that his superior officers let him go.

Once the thought of death had seriously crossed his mind, he could not shake it, and he wanted to marry Mary Haley before he died. He told the story many years later to his friend, the authoress Anna Jameson.

F. said, that if his request was granted, he would be again at head-quarters within three days; if refused, he would go without leave. "For," said he, "I was desperate, and the truth was, ma'am, there was a little girl that I loved, and I knew that if I could marry her before I was killed, and I a captain, she would have the pension of a captain's widow."

The leave of absence was granted. Just how he got to Adolphustown, 220 miles from the Niagara frontier, is a mystery.

His granddaughter says, "Landing at the Carrying Place, he rode sixty miles to the church door."

If he did travel by water, he defied Chauncey's fleet which had finally sailed from Sackett's Harbour and appeared off the Niagara River on August 5. Chauncey then sailed off to Kingston to stop the movement of troops and provisions to the frontier, but he left small war ships to blockade Fort George. On August 14, Sir George Prevost complained, "the Naval Ascendancy possessed by the Enemy on Lake Ontario enables him to perform in two days what our Troops going from Kingston to reinforce the Right Division required from Sixteen to Twenty of severe marching to accomplish . . . the route from Kingston to the Niagara frontier exceeds Two Hundred and Fifty Miles."

Throughout all of August, enemy ships hovered before Fort George. It would be possible for bateaux to get away and follow the shoreline to York and the Carrying Place but it is hard to imagine FitzGibbon making such a trip to and fro in just three days.

Anna Jameson says, "FitzGibbon mounted his horse, rode a hundred and fifty miles in an exceedingly short time, married his little girl, and returned the day following to his duties, and to fight another battle, in which however he was not killed." Actually it is close to 200 miles from Fort Erie to the Carrying Place and another thirty miles to Adolphustown. If he did ride a horse there and back in three days he moved with the legendary speed of a pony express. At any rate, he got there. Mary got there by travelling thirty miles from Kingston with the Reverend George Okill Stuart who would marry them. It is likely that Drummond took advantage of FitzGibbon's trip to send despatches with him which Mary and the Reverend Stuart would then carry on to Kingston.

Their marriage certificate, which is filed in the Synod Office of St. George's Cathedral in Kingston, states that

> James FitzGibbon, Captain in his
> Majesty's Glengarry Lt. Infantry Fencibles
> was married to Mary Haley (by licence)
> by me George Okill Stuart
> on the 14th day of August, 1814.

Mary Agnes FitzGibbon says her grandfather said goodbye to his bride on the church steps and rode back to keep his word to his colonel.

The enemy evacuated Fort Erie early this forenoon, having first blown up the works and in every other respect completely destroyed and dismantled the place, an event on which I offer Your Excellency my sincere congratulations. Captain FitzGibbon rode through every part of the place, in which the enemy had left nothing except ten or twelve kegs of damaged musket ball cartridges.

Sir Gordon Drummond to Sir George Prevost, Falls of Niagara, November 5, 1814.

14

Even on the fastest horse, FitzGibbon could not have reached Fort Erie for the attack made by the British in the wee small hours of August 15. Drummond launched his men in three columns against the fort. One unit waded along the Lake Erie shore to get into the rear of the camp and was entirely captured. Two of the columns led by Colonels Drummond and Hercules Scott fought desperately to gain the northeast bastion. Suddenly, at about daybreak, the northeast bastion exploded as powder stored in a magazine ignited. The result was incredible confusion and instant death for many of the British. Those who survived ran for their lives. Among those who died in Fort Erie were Colonel William Drummond, nephew of General Drummond, and Colonel Hercules Scott of the 103rd.

FitzGibbon came back from his wedding to a less-than-merry camp. Letters written from General Drummond to Prevost in late August are full of worry and invariably concerned about provisions. As long as Chauncey ruled the water, flour and pork could not be brought in to feed the troops. The road between

Kingston and Niagara was so poor that it was not practical to send loaded wagons over it; only bateaux could be employed to move stores. On August 18 Drummond wrote of his army's needs: "Its wants in provisions, ammunition and stores of every kind, have become so alarmingly great and urgent that nothing but the assistance of the whole of H.M. squadron on Lake Ontario can enable it to continue its operations." Again on August 21 he wrote of their need for ammunition, artillery, and artificers to build some sort of shelters for the men: "We possess no means of making anything like adequate preparations for covering the troops which it may be necessary to retain on this frontier during the approaching winter."

Under "Barracks" Drummond wrote: "Stores of every description, particularly stoves, of which there are abundance at Kingston ... It is by the squadron *alone* that relief can reach us, and from the accounts I have lately received of the state of forwardness of the new ship, I really begin to fear that relief by this mode may not reach us in time." Two officers were sent through the countryside to induce each farmer to thresh his grain early and sell from five to twelve bushels to the army to enable it to hold out.

In answer to Drummond's cry of distress, Major-General Stovin at Kingston sent forward a large detachment of bateaux laden with provisions and stores. Another stroke of good luck was the disappearance of the war vessels blockading Fort George. Drummond hurried the schooner *Vincent* off to York carrying prisoners and the sick, and sent after it the schooner *Netley* and the brig *Charwell*. At York the schooners waited for the 97th Regiment but before it arrived in Kingston on September 10, the two American ships were back. The 97th were reduced to walking to Niagara, and further provisions would have to move by bateaux.

In September, FitzGibbon was employed carrying despatches to Kingston. He may have been sent post-haste to warn Stovin that the war ships were back. Perhaps the speed of his wedding trip recommended him for the service or perhaps his superiors were kind enough to arrange that he would have some time with his wife. His granddaughter says he travelled back to Niagara with Major-General Stovin on September 17. Drummond had requested that Stovin join him on the frontier as his own health was still not good.

The changing news from the rest of the war brought shock waves of hope and dismay alternately to Kingston and Niagara. In mid-summer an American fleet of six vessels had attacked Michilimackinac but Lieutenant-Colonel McDougall with 140 regulars, plus militia and Indians, defended his post so well that they sailed away on August 5, the British flag still flying proudly over the northwest. Late in August, Canadians had been almost as stunned as Americans to learn that a British force under Major-General Ross and Rear-Admiral Cockburn had moved up the Patuxent River on August 24 and burned the Capitol, the public buildings, and the presidential residence in Washington. Retaliation for the burning of York was complete.

In early September, the British fleet and army moved up Chesapeake Bay toward the city of Baltimore. As they bombarded that well-fortified city, a young American lawyer wrote what would become the American national anthem.

While Washington burned, the peace talks which would eventually end this war were already underway at Ghent. The commissioners first met on August 8 and at first made little progress.

The next news to reach Upper Canada was from Lake Champlain and was the worst the Canadians had heard for some time. On September 1, Sir George Prevost led an army of 10,000 into American territory. He had with him some of the best generals from Wellington's army. By September 6 they had reached Plattsburgh and awaited the cooperation of the British fleet on Lake Champlain, under Captain Downie. British and Americans each had four ships but Downie's large ship, the H.M.S. *Confiance*, was unfinished. What happened was that Prevost rushed Downie into action before he was properly ready and, when cheering American spectators indicated a British defeat on the water, Prevost withdrew his formidable army which was already across the Saranac River and on the verge of taking Plattsburgh. Wellington's generals were furious; the stunned army fell back and returned in disgrace to Lower Canada.

Early in September, rain started to fall on the camp at Fort Erie, and it rained for thirteen consecutive days. Tiger Dunlop described the army's situation as "rather a bivouac than a camp, the troops sheltering themselves under some branches of trees that only collected the scattered drops of rain, and sent them down in a stream on the heads of the inhabitants, and as it rained incessantly for two months, neither clothes nor bedding could be kept dry."

Although the army of 1814 was far more healthy than it had been at the end of the summer in 1813, sickness began to appear in September. It was inevitable that it would spread as the men were now camped in what amounted to a shallow lake. Drummond began to talk of falling back to higher ground on the Chippawa, yet he was reluctant to go and the work on the third battery went on. General Brown in Fort Erie began to see that the newest battery, "would rake obliquely the whole American encampment," and he determined to take it. FitzGibbon and Major-General Stovin arrived back from Kingston just before Brown's army attacked the British batteries on September 17.

Suddenly at about three o'clock in the afternoon, 1,600 Americans—militia and regulars—sprang out of the woods to attack the blockhouse at No. 3 Battery. Taking both blockhouse and battery from De Watteville's troops on guard, the Americans advanced to capture Battery No. 2. By the time they reached the third battery, the British regiments were out in force and a wild fight was underway.

The Glengarry Regiment was in the thick of it. In despatches written later by Major-General De Watteville, their part is described: "Lieut.-Col. Pearson, with the Glengarry Light Infantry under Lieut.-Col. Battersby, pushed forward by the centre road and carried with great gallantry the new entrenchment, then in full possession of the enemy." Brown had brought up his reserve but, even so, was unable to take the battery. Under heavy fire he was forced to pull back his troops. Later Drummond wrote, "I myself witnessed the good order and spirit with which the Glengarry Light Infantry, under Lieut.-Col. Battersby pushed into the wood, and by their superior fire drove back the enemy's light troops." By five o'clock it was over and the British line reestablished as it had been, but seventy-nine Americans and about one hundred British had been killed and almost another thousand wounded.

Drummond decided the time had come to move back toward the Chippawa, the dreadful appearance of typhoid fever in camp hastening his decision. Drummond described the condition of his men as one of extreme wretchedness: "Their present camp literally resembles a lake in the midst of a thick wood." At eight o'clock on the evening of September 21, they reached the site of their new camp and bivouacked for the night under torrents of rain.

On October 5, General Izard marched 4,000 soldiers from Lake Champlain into Lewiston. Izard was soon in command at Fort Erie with a total force of 6,000 men. Drummond began to despair of his situation and lashed out in anger at Sir James Yeo for not daring to bring him the troops now in the country but without transportation to reach the frontier. He wrote: "I have, however, ceased to reckon upon any relief depending on the squadron. ... Should any disaster happen to this division ... His Majesty's naval commander will in my opinion, have much to answer for."

Meanwhile FitzGibbon and his Glengarries, posted in advance of the army, were busy at a pushing back and forth type of warfare as Americans advanced toward the British camp at Chippawa and were repeatedly repulsed.

On October 18, more than 1,500 Americans were met by the Glengarries, the 82nd Regiment, and the 100th Regiment near the mills on Lyon's Creek. Afterwards Colonel Meyers, who led the British force, wrote: "The conduct of the Glengarry Light Infantry during this campaign has been so conspicuous that Lieutenant-Colonel Battersby and the officers and men of that corps can receive little further from any report of mine, but on this occasion I cannot refrain from adding my humble tribute of praise to their well-earned fame."

At last, on October 17, Sir James Yeo's fleet appeared at the mouth of the Niagara River. His new three-decked super-sized ship the *St. Lawrence* had finally sailed, bristling with 112 guns. Chauncey's fleet, as well as a small army under Brown, had already gone off to Sackett's Harbour for fear of what Yeo and his big-gunned ship might do there. The arrival of the British fleet helped convince General Izard that maybe the game was up. The approach of a Canadian winter also helped to cool the ardour of the American attackers. In the afternoon of October 20, Izard started his army moving back toward Fort Erie. Finally, a report reached Drummond that the Americans were evacuating the fort, and he quickly sent Captain FitzGibbon with a small party of Glengarries to take a close look.

Fitz left his party in the woods and rode on alone. He stopped close to the fort and listened to the silence. No sound reached him but the wind rustling some leaves still on the November trees. An almost eerie atmosphere hung over the fort, and he was sure it was empty. Waving back at his men to stay put, he rode cautiously into the fort. The place was in ruins. They had destroyed, dismantled, or blown up all the works inside the fort before they left. Nothing remained but ten or twelve kegs of damaged musket ball and cartridge.

Sitting his horse in the midst of the empty chaos, he experienced a great wave of elation that spread a wide grin over his face. This moment would always stick in his mind as the end of the war, although peace would not be official until March. Fort Erie was empty. Not one American remained this side of the Niagara. He thought about Mary and the future he had not dared to plan. Maybe after all, he had survived this crazy war.

He rode back outside the fort, let out a wild Irish yell and motioned his men to come on in.

15

This family compact surround the Lieutenant-Governor, and mould him, like wax, to their will; they fill every office with their relatives, dependants, and partisans; – they are paymasters, receivers, auditors, kings, Lords, and Commons!

William Lyon Mackenzie, *Sketches of Upper Canada and the United States* (London, 1833).

It was 1834. Twenty years had passed, years in which Fitz had tackled civilian life much as he would another battle. But it was a battle more difficult to win because his enemies were the times he lived in, the political system, and, above all, his friends in the Family Compact.

It was inevitable that his allegiance should be with the Compact, that close-knit body of friends and relatives that ruled Upper Canada. The Compact was composed first of an inner circle of Loyalists who had fled the American Revolution, then of sons of Loyalists and immigrants who had come from Great Britain about the turn of the century. These men had fought together in the War of 1812 and imbibed a life-long hatred of American ideas of democracy and reform.

A roll call of the powerful men of York reads like a list for a reunion of veterans of the war, and their shared experience helped bond them together. John Strachan, who personally defied General Dearborn when the Americans took York, was archdeacon of York in 1834 and a central figure in the Family

Compact. John Beverley Robinson, one of the eager young men of York who accompanied Brock to Detroit, became Attorney-General after Macdonell fell with Brock at Queenston. By 1834 Robinson was Chief Justice of Upper Canada and, next to Strachan, the most influential man in the province. William Allan, too, had been an officer in the War of 1812. He was to become the financial brain of the Compact, a wealthy merchant, President of the Bank of Upper Canada, a member of both the Legislative and Executive Councils. Christopher Hagerman, aide-de-camp to Sir George Prevost during the war, was Solicitor-General in 1834.

Other familiar names found places in the outer circles of Compact influence. William Jarvis, who saw Brock fall at Queenston, became sheriff of the Home District. Thomas Ridout, the young man who stole onions and fence rails for the commissariat at Niagara, helped to organize the Bank of Upper Canada and was its first cashier. William Hamilton Merritt, FitzGibbon's hard-riding comrade of Green Tiger days, became a dynamic political leader and promoter of the Welland Canal. Tiger Dunlop, who brought his colourful personality to the rainy days before the fall of Fort Erie, made financial hay with the Canada Company which owned large tracts of land near Goderich.

Allied against the Family Compact were immigrants of the 1820's, many of whom brought radical ideas into this stronghold of Tory reaction, and immigrants from the United States who had American democracy inherent in their characters and outlook.

Anna Jameson, who came from England in 1833, described the leaders of Upper Canada as "a stiff-necked gentry who have formed a petty kingdom in a raw lake port." Her husband, who had come to serve as Attorney-General, was nominally one of them, but this did not prevent Anna from seeing things the way they were.

The allegiance to king and country of the sheriffs, magistrates, militia officers and customs-collectors who formed the outer circles of the Compact was equally strong, but their rewards were certainly less than those of the ruling elite. It was among this group that FitzGibbon found himself. He held a variety of jobs, all directly connected to government, all poorly paid. He had remained with his regiment in York until it was disbanded in 1816, then taken a job in the office of the adjutant-general of militia. He was a land agent briefly, justice of the peace, administrator of the Oath of Allegiance in the Legislative Assembly, and, by 1822, assistant adjutant-general of militia. In 1826 he was gazetted Colonel of the West York Militia of Canada and resigned as assistant adjutant-general. In 1827 he became clerk of the House of Assembly.

James had first gone into debt when appointed to the adjutancy of the 49th in 1806, in order to buy his horse and uniform, and he remained in debt almost to his dying day. According to many old friends who have written of Fitz, he was generous to a fault and many times went even deeper in debt to help a friend whose situation seemed worse than his own. He also lived beyond his means, in the style of his friends and co-workers but without the private funds they often had.

His home in 1834 was a two-storey house on eighteen acres of land on the southwest corner of what is now Queen Street and Spadina Avenue in Toronto. It sat well back on the lot, and graceful willow trees grew near the road. There was a bowling green on the lawn surrounded by spacious gardens filled with fruit and flowers. The gardener's wages no doubt added to Fitz-Gibbon's debt.

His first years with Mary were very happy. They were young, in love, thrilled by the joyous daily details of life without war. They had happy, healthy children; first a daughter Mary, then Charles, William, George, and James. But what happened afterwards is harder to explain. They had twelve more children, and none of them survived. No records remain to explain how they died. Cholera raged in York in 1832 and again in 1834. These were days when many children died of childhood diseases like scarlet fever, diphtheria, and smallpox. But twelve seems an incredible number to lose when one considers that their first five were healthy. By the 1830's Fitz speaks of his wife as delicate and unwell. When one considers that Mary was continually bearing and burying children, one wonders how she could remain sane, let alone well. Yet there were happy days for the family, too. Both James and Mary did everything in their power to see that their children were educated and cultured. In the 1830's the boys are described walking or racing to Upper Canada College with Fitz as he went in the same direction to the House of Assembly. They were bright-eyed lads, strong and physically fit like their father and with his same passion for life and success.

FitzGibbon himself had many friends. His favourites were those who had shared the war with him. He was known as a superb teller of stories, a warm-hearted, generous man who would do anything for a friend or a cause he believed in. Many of his friends belonged to the Masonic Order as Fitz had been a Mason since he was stationed in Quebec in 1803. For a number of years he was Provincial Grand Master of the Order.

Anna Jameson, who was very fond of Fitz, saw the poetic side of his nature and repeats a story he told which delighted her. One day as he walked along in Toronto he heard the singing of a lark although there are no larks in this country.

> So, ma'am, when I heard the voice of the bird in the air, I looked, by the natural instinct, up to the heavens, though I knew it could not be there, and then on this side, and then on that, and sure enough at last I saw the little creature perched on its sod of turf in a little cage, and there it kept trilling and warbling away, and there I stood stock-still — listening with my heart. Well, I don't know what it was at all that came over me, but everything seemed to change before my eyes, and it was in poor Ireland I was again, and my home all about me, and I was again a wild slip of a boy, lying on my back on the hill-side above my mother's cabin, and watching, as I used to do, the lark singing and soaring over my head, and I straining my eye to follow her, till she melted into the blue sky, and there, ma'am — would you believe it? — I stood like an old fool listening to the bird's song, lost, as in a dream, and there I think I could have stood till this day.

According to his granddaughter he had a habit of "interfering in whatever occurred within his cognizance whenever there appeared the remotest chance of such interference being for good, whether it was any of his business or not." It was inevitable that a man who put so much passion into what he believed should have enemies too. By 1834 he had one particular enemy. William Lyon Mackenzie, who published a radical newspaper, *The Colonial Advocate*, ranted and railed against everything Fitz-Gibbon believed in.

Although politically on opposite sides, the two men were oddly alike. Both had been born poor and had educated themselves with fanatic determination. Both had an immense capacity for work. Mackenzie could, and often did, work all through the night, pouring into printer's ink all the anger and frustration he felt toward the Family Compact. Anna Jameson wrote of Fitz: "With so much overflowing benevolence and fearless energy of character, and all the eccentricity, and sensibility, and poetry, and headlong courage of his country, you cannot wonder that this brave and worthy man interests me; unluckily, I can see him seldom, his life being one of almost unremitting toil."

Both men were gifted orators. FitzGibbon used his gift to entertain or, on several occasions, to restore peace and order. In 1823 he was sent by the Governor to Perth where riots had broken out between Protestant and Catholic Irish. His gift of speech was even more eloquent in Gaelic and he soon had a mob of angry men quieted as they listened to him. In 1826 he was sent to Peterborough where similar trouble threatened, and again the magic of his Irish oratory saved the situation.

Mackenzie, on the other hand, used his colourful command of words to arouse and incite the people against the government. He described the Family Compact as "official fungi, more numerous and pestilential than the marshes and quagmires that encircle Toronto." Settlers who normally had little time to enquire into politics could not ignore this little Scotsman who bent over their ploughshares and poured out volumes of abuse against the Strachans and Robinsons and Hagermans and their like. When the personal fortune of a farmer was less than good, the words of Mackenzie rang in his head and he began to believe that maybe the government really was to blame.

Both men led charmed lives, had incredible energy, and seemed impervious to personal danger. When cholera struck York in 1832 and again in 1834, both Mackenzie and FitzGibbon could be seen removing the sick to the hospital by cart and driving cartloads of dead to be buried.

By 1834 Mackenzie and Fitz had clashed repeatedly. In 1831 Mackenzie had been charged with "gross, scandalous, and malicious libel" and expelled from the House of Assembly. He was immediately re-elected and again expelled and then three times more refused his seat in the House. The January 1832 election revealed the growing popularity of Mackenzie. The poll at the Red Lion Tavern had closed by three o'clock with 119 votes cast for Mackenzie, only one for his opponent. In the large ballroom of the Red Lion, his supporters cheered and lauded Mackenzie and presented him with a huge gold medal and chain. Then in a procession of 134 sleighs led by highland pipers they paraded their hero-agitator into town. On one sleigh a printing press, kept warm by a small furnace beneath it, turned out New Year messages which boys threw to the crowd.

Things on both sides were reaching fever pitch by March 23 when Mackenzie spoke at an open-air meeting. Government sympathizers gathered and began to stone him. The mob was also threatening to burn Mackenzie in effigy and attack the office of the *Colonial Advocate*. Men were about to rush the building when FitzGibbon arrived, forced his way to the front, seized two of the ring-leaders and dragged them to the nearby jail. He was soon back, calling in a clear, loud voice for law and order, while Mackenzie's excited lungs demanded that soldiers be called out.

FitzGibbon said there was no need for that if Mackenzie would just retire. Mackenzie refused and Fitz threatened to put him in jail, too. Mackenzie said he wouldn't dare as he was a Member of Parliament. Fitz grabbed him and was dragging him in the direction of the jail when two other Members of Parliament appeared and he gave Mackenzie into their care instead. But, just outside his own house, Mackenzie tried again to address the crowd. Fitz opened the door of the house, took him by the shoulders, pushed him inside and shut the door. Thus ended Mackenzie's speech.

Later that night the Governor, Sir John Colborne, summoned Fitz to say that others were urging that he call out the troops to guard the city that night. "For God's sake, sir, do nothing of the kind. Give no orders whatever." FitzGibbon explained that this was just what Mackenzie wanted. He had been outnumbered and beaten tonight, but calling out the troops would make him a martyr by tomorrow. Colborne took FitzGibbon's advice.

Two years later, in 1834, the town of York became the city of Toronto. William Lyon Mackenzie had been elected mayor by a vote of the aldermen, to the disgust of many staunch old Family Compact types. On July 29, a noisy meeting was held to discuss city debt and the necessity of a heavy tax being levied. The meeting was adjourned to be held the following day in the market place.

What happened then was an accident but it would stamp the image of Mackenzie on FitzGibbon's life in colours of horror and grief. The whole city was excited about the meeting, and young and old turned out. A lot of boys, including FitzGibbon's sons, managed to find standing room on a balcony over some butchers' stalls. When Sheriff Jarvis spoke in support of a vote of censure against Mackenzie he said, "I care no more for Mackenzie than," looking up he added dramatically, "than that crow!"

The crowd stamped and cheered and the balcony collapsed, dumping the people who were on it to the ground. Several suffered broken bones. But far more dreadful was the fate of the few impaled upon the great hooks of the butchers' stalls beneath. FitzGibbon's third son, George, was one of these. Fitz, stunned with grief, carried the boy home to his horrified mother. He was dreadfully injured, and James and Mary knew he would not live. Fitz had seen men die of awful wounds during the war but this was his own son, a boy of sixteen with his whole life before him. FitzGibbon's whole being cried out against cruel fate.

FitzGibbon's granddaughter describes George as "a fine promising lad of sixteen, whose ready wit and brilliant sallies were the life of his school-mates, and whose abilities promised future success at the Bar, the profession to which he had been early destined by his father."

George only lived a few hours more but in such pain that James and Mary could only be glad to see him go. The scar left on their lives never completely healed. His mother's physical health steadily deteriorated while Fitz himself seemed to bear the abrasion mentally. He worked even harder, driving himself for king and country; he worried incessantly about the forces of democracy and rebellion insidiously at work to undermine the political system he believed in. In some deep recess of his mind he always linked Mackenzie with the terrible death of his son. As the pressures and anxieties of his life and the political turmoil around him increased, that red-wigged agitator became for Fitz a personal obsession.

16

> With regard to his services in 1837, I have no doubt that his earnest conviction before the outbreak that violence would be attempted, and the measures of precaution which he spontaneously took in consequence of that impression, were the means of saving the Government and the loyal inhabitants of Toronto from being for a time at least at the mercy of the rebels; and I believe the most disastrous consequences would have followed the surprise which Colonel Fitz-Gibbon's vigilance prevented.
>
> John Robinson, enclosed in a note from the Lord Bishop of Toronto, dated London, 83 Sackville Street, August 16, 1839.

By the first of December 1837, FitzGibbon was certain that there would be a rebellion in Upper Canada. The November 24 issue of Mackenzie's newspaper had published what was, in fact, a constitution for the new state of Upper Canada. Throughout the countryside, Mackenzie had a network of vigilance committees that could serve as a military set-up in time of war. Meanwhile, there was news from Lower Canada of a successful *patriote* revolt led by Papineau; this would certainly boost the morale of Mackenzie's rebels.

The writing was on the wall, but it was the bad luck of Upper Canada to have a lieutenant-governor who couldn't read it. Since Sir John Colborne had been transferred to Lower Canada as the new Governor General, he had been replaced in Upper Canada by Sir Francis Bond Head, a blue-eyed, curly-haired, rather handsome and winsome man, but curiously lacking in commonsense. For weeks FitzGibbon had been trying to convince this obstinate man that they were going to have a rebellion in Upper Canada. When Sir John Colborne had written to ask Sir Francis whether he could spare any troops for Lower Canada, Sir Francis replied that he would gladly send them all. When the last detachment moved from Penetanguishene through Toronto, on their way to the city of Quebec, FitzGibbon begged Head to keep them. Sir Francis' lofty reply was, "I do not apprehend a rebellion in Upper Canada."

Back in 1834 Fitz had spoken to Colborne of his fears for the future. Colborne agreed that FitzGibbon should form a corps of young Toronto men which he would drill during the summer months. The corps was limited to seventy because they had seventy rifles available. During the summers from 1834 to 1837, Fitz drilled the boys twice a week. His granddaughter says, "Perhaps the happiest hours of these years were spent in this labour of love. He was a soldier before everything. He loved the very rattle of accoutrements." Now in 1837, these seventy young men, drilled by an old pro, could be of real importance to this city left without a regular soldier.

The state of the city's militia was further evidence of Head's contrariness. When Fitz had transferred this year from the York militia to the First Regiment of the city of Toronto, he found twenty vacancies and went to Head asking him to appoint officers to fill these posts. Head refused to do anything until spring. Six thousand stand of small arms and ammunition had recently been sent from Kingston to Toronto and were placed by Francis Bond Head in the market hall where he had only two constables guarding them. Fitz offered to use his corps of young volunteers to guard these arms. Head, of course, refused.

By this time Fitz was driven near distraction. But he was never one to give up. If he could not do something official to guard this city, he would do it unofficially through personal friends, militiamen, co-workers and fellow Masons. He sat down and wrote a list of names, 126 men in all, whom he knew to be loyal citizens. With list in hand, he went to Head, not to ask, but to tell. He, FitzGibbon would warn each of the men on this list to be prepared to come armed to the Parliament Buildings at any hour of the day or night when they heard the college bell ring an alarm. He would also arrange that the cathedral bells be rung to warn loyal citizens east of Yonge Street. Sir Francis

Bond Head was stunned, but FitzGibbon did not stop talking long enough to let him say anything. "For the doing of this I desire to have your Excellency's sanction, but permit me to tell your Excellency that, whether you give me leave or not, I mean to do it." Sir Francis, overwhelmed by the determined passion of FitzGibbon, consented. FitzGibbon scurried off before the Governor could change his mind.

On the second of December, a Saturday, a man made his way into town along Yonge Street Road and sought out James Fitz-Gibbon. He was a fellow Mason and brought confidential information that pikes were being forged at Lount's blacksmith shop at Holland Landing, and men were secretly drilling every day in North York. FitzGibbon hurried with the news to Sir Francis. After a six-hour discussion, Head and his council could not agree whether the news was important or not. Head complained that the information the man brought was third- or fourth-hand. Fitz had at least one supporter. The Honourable William Allan rose and said, "What would you have, gentlemen? Do you expect the rebels will come and give you information at first hand?" Laughter broke the tension briefly. Allan finished his speech, "I agree in every word spoken here today by Colonel FitzGibbon, and think that an hour should not be lost without preparing ourselves for defence."

But nothing was done until Monday morning. Then Fitz-Gibbon was summoned to Sir Francis and handed a militia general order which appointed him Adjutant-General of Militia. As that post was already filled by Colonel Coffin, Fitz declined. But knowing the need of the moment and disorganization of the militia department, he finally consented to be "Acting Adjutant-General."

FitzGibbon had an extremely busy day. By night he was more than ever convinced of the imminence of attack. He and several friends decided to keep vigil at his office in the Parliament Buildings all night. At about ten o'clock, something having alarmed him further, Fitz went again to Government House. The Governor was in bed and Fitz insisted that his sister get him up. He knew Head now regarded him as a personal irritant as noxious as poison ivy, but he did not care.

What the two men said to one another is not recorded but Head went back to bed. Within an hour, while the Governor slept peacefully, FitzGibbon had definite information that the rebels were moving on Toronto.

At Montgomery's Tavern, seven miles north on Yonge Street, a mass of rebels had assembled ready to march on the city. Three loyal Tories from Richmond Hill decided to risk riding through the pickets. Colonel Moodie was shot dead, Captain Hugh Stewart was captured, but a third man named Brooke got through and brought the news to the city.

Fitz had no time for Head now. One of his rifle corps was sent post-haste to ring the college bells. Fitz jumped on a horse and galloped through the west end of Toronto shouting out to the men to assemble at the Parliament Buildings. Then he rode to the church because the bells were not yet ringing.

Next he was back at City Hall, giving directions that the arms now stored there be distributed to the men as they arrived. He and two students then rode up Yonge Street to see what they could see. They rode as far as Rosedale (the estate of Sheriff William Jarvis) and saw no sign of rebels. Here Fitz decided to turn back and arranged for a picket to be posted there. The two boys, one a son of Major Brock of the 49th Regiment, wanted to ride on to reconnoitre Montgomery's Tavern. FitzGibbon let them go, but he was nervous for their safety. Suddenly out of the night rode John Powell and a Mr. McDonald, also rebel hunting. FitzGibbon urged them to overtake the two boys.

When Fitz got back into Toronto he went to Government House. Head was actually up and Fitz was more than a little surprised to find him talking to John Powell whom he had just left riding north on Yonge Street Road. Powell, red in the face and out of breath, had a remarkable story to tell. Before he and McDonald could reach the boys, the two had been taken prisoners by Mackenzie, a Captain Anderson, who was to be the military leader of the rebels, and three other rebels. Powell and McDonald soon ran into the party and became prisoners, too.

Mackenzie had then left Anderson and Sheppard to take their prisoners to Montgomery's Tavern while he rode toward Toronto. But, nearing Montgomery's, Powell, who was forced to ride in front, suddenly delved for a pistol hidden in his coat, wheeled his horse and shot Anderson in the neck. Anderson fell dead from his horse and Powell rode pell-mell for Toronto. Afraid he was pursued, the portly Powell abandoned his horse at Davenport Road and ran puffing across Queen's Park and down College (now University) Avenue to Government House where he had great trouble getting Mrs. Dalrymple to awaken her brother a second time. But by the time Fitz arrived, Sir Francis was convinced — in fact was close to panic — and ready to hurry off to City Hall with him.

It was a wild night in Toronto, FitzGibbon said later; one of the most anxious he ever spent. Judge Jones had already formed a picket and marched it out Yonge Street Road to the toll gate. But here at City Hall Fitz had a mob from which to make an army, and he had no way to know who was friend or foe. Many of these men clamouring for arms might go directly to join Mackenzie once they had weapons. But by Tuesday morning, he and Assistant Adjutant-General Foster had the men formed in platoons in the market square. A 6-pounder gun stood loaded in front of City Hall. As the day went on men worked to barricade the windows of City Hall, the Bank of Upper Canada, the Parliament Buildings, Osgoode Hall, and Government House, with two-inch planks loop-holed for musketry.

FitzGibbon had galloped out in the morning with a party of seven to check a rumour that the rebels had fortified Montgomery's Tavern. What he saw convinced him instead that he could take the 6-pounder, 300 of the 500 men he had, and surprise and suppress the rebels before any damage was done Toronto. Sir Francis refused. His answer to Fitz was, "No, sir, I will not fight them on their ground; they must fight me on mine." Fitz tried to warn him of the danger that Mackenzie's men would set fire to the city; he urged him not to risk valuable property and lives.

Later in the day they clashed on another matter. Judge Jones had brought his Yonge Street picket back into the city Tuesday morning and Fitz was forming another for Tuesday night. Sir Francis saw him and forbade him to send a man out. "We cannot defend the city, we have not men enough; let us defend our posts. . . . It is my positive order that you do not leave this building yourself."

Fitz replied, "I pray of your Excellency not to lay those imperative orders upon me for I ought to be in many places, and I ought to be allowed to exercise a discretionary power where you are not near to give me orders."

Seizing Fitz by the arm with both hands, the Governor exclaimed, "If you go through the city as you have heretofore done, you will be taken prisoner! If we lose you, what shall we do?"

FitzGibbon ignored him, took Sheriff Jarvis with a picket up Yonge Street, then came back and told Head what he had done. That night the picket stopped a motley force of rebels who had been sent toward the city for the purpose of setting it on fire.

When it was almost midnight, Sir Francis suddenly decided they should remove the spare arms to the Parliament Buildings which were farther away and less liable to be burned. Fitz was horrified. In the confusion and darkness of night, the Governor wanted each man to lay down his loaded weapon and march with a half-dozen unloaded arms to the Parliament Buildings. The situation could get entirely out of control if a spy informed Mackenzie what was going on or if some of the men carrying weapons happened to be disloyal. But Sir Francis had lost the last argument to FitzGibbon and was determined with all his might to win this one. The night was saved by the arrival of Allan MacNab, Speaker of the House of Assembly, with sixty men from Hamilton. Fitz could now convince the Governor that with MacNab's men he could guard all approaches and the arms would be safe where they were until morning.

On Wednesday, Sir Francis appointed MacNab to the command of the militia of the Home District. FitzGibbon, without knowing the Governor had given the command to someone else, attempted on Wednesday night to argue Head into an attack next morning. With nothing settled, Fitz who had not slept since Sunday, went home briefly, then back to the Parliament Buildings where he slept until four o'clock Thursday morning. The first thing he did then was to draft a plan for attack. Soon Fitz was summoned to a room nearby where Sir Francis was still in bed. MacNab was there with Judge Macaulay and the Honourable John Macaulay. The Governor said he found himself in a painful position, having as rivals before him two officers of equal zeal, of equal bravery, and of equal talent, competing for the command.

MacNab's military experience, apart from the militia, was limited to a cadetship for one year and the part of a year he had served as ensign. Fitz said nothing at all but if his face expressed his feelings Head must have withered a little. Finally the Governor first asked to be alone with MacNab, then summoned Fitz and the Macaulays and said MacNab had released him from his promise and the command was FitzGibbon's.

By twelve noon on December 7, 1837, Fitz had his grand army ready to march. There were 920 men. The main body, 600 strong, was led up Yonge Street by FitzGibbon, MacNab, and Sir Francis. A left wing of 200 men moved up College Avenue and on to the north by side roads. A right wing led by Colonel Jarvis marched along east of Yonge Street. It was a fine bright day, and two bands raised the spirits of the soldiers and the people who watched. Many townspeople joined, as they would in a parade, and marched out to the scene of battle.

The battle was one of the shortest in history. The rebel force that met FitzGibbon's 920 men was somewhere between 400 and 600 men. Only one man, Ludwig Wideman, was killed in the actual battle although eleven Patriots were wounded and at least four died later. Fitz's army suffered five wounded.

Within minutes the rebels were fleeing in all directions. The one FitzGibbon desired most to catch was Mackenzie. But the agile little Scotsman had abandoned his horse and disappeared into the woods. (In the December cold with the entire Tory countryside hunting him, Mackenzie would manage to hide and slide his way to Niagara and cross into the United States.)

When FitzGibbon turned back to Montgomery's he found the tavern in flames. He had already met a party of forty men heading north with orders to burn the house of David Gibson, one of Mackenzie's major supporters. Fitz did not believe the order could have been given and hurried on to check with Sir Francis. The Governor and main body of the army were now on their way back to Toronto. When FitzGibbon reached Sir Francis and tried to object to burning Gibson's house, the Governor's words were "Stop; hear me—let Gibson's house be burned forthwith, and let the militia be kept here until it be burned." Then the Governor galloped away, leaving Fitz with the burden of carrying out the cruel order.

After the rebellion Sir Francis published his *Narrative* and distorted the facts like this: "The Militia advanced in pursuit of the rebels about four miles till they reached the house of one of the principal ringleaders, Mr. Gibson, which residence it would have been impossible to have saved, and it was consequently burned to the ground."

An angry FitzGibbon wrote to Lord Glenelg, Colonial Secretary, and pointed out the lies (there were others) in Head's account. Lord Glenelg made Sir Francis admit the lie by adding a footnote after "burned to the ground." The footnote read, "by my especial order."

FitzGibbon's granddaughter says that had the order been given him in private, he would not have obeyed. But his military training made it imperative that an order given by his commander-in-chief in front of his men be obeyed. Fitz had first ordered his field officer to carry out the Governor's command, but the man implored him, "For God's sake, Colonel FitzGibbon, do not send me to carry out this order."

"If you are not willing to obey orders, you had better go home and retire from the militia."

"I am very willing to obey orders, but if I burn that house, I shall be shot from behind one of these fences, for I have to come over this road almost every day in the week."

FitzGibbon let the man go and took the party himself to burn the house.

This should have been FitzGibbon's finest hour. He had just saved the city of Toronto. But thanks to the machinations of Sir Francis Bond Head, he had come to his lowest performance. He knew David Gibson, knew he would be fleeing to the States so that he would not end up in jail facing a death sentence. Mrs. Gibson and four young children would be alone to face the Canadian winter. And there he stood burning their house.

By the time Fitz reached his own house that night he was so

exhausted that his children had to help him dismount. His mental state was even worse. The sleepless days and nights, the terrible anxiety, the eternal frustration of dealing with Head, and the final meanness of having to burn Dave Gibson's house, had left him sick in body, mind, and soul. Nor was there any happy comfort in his home. Mary was sick. His youngest child was dying. Fitz himself was unable to get out of bed, but he sent a message to Sir Francis Bond Head resigning the appointment as Adjutant-General.

Sir Francis accepted and appointed Colonel Allan MacNab to succeed him.

It was at once the most successful as well as the most disastrous
year of my life. What occurred
then enabled me to accomplish
something towards the saving of
the city of Toronto and the over-
throw of the rebels – having no
thought of reward, other than the
saving of bloodshed – and the
spontaneous and unanimous
vote of my fellow-citizens to reward me for what I had done,
roused such hopes of freedom
from my pecuniary difficulties
that their defeat well-nigh imper-
illed my reason.

James FitzGibbon, letter to Sir
Augustus d'Este in 1844.

17

The rebellion of 1837 was over. Sir Francis Bond Head
was recalled. Convinced that he would be murdered en route, he
left the country in March, furtively, like a criminal. Pretending
to be bound for Montreal, he and Judge Jones crossed to the
United States from Kingston, paddling a small boat from one
ice floe to another. They arrived at Watertown and stayed at the
Mansion House where, of all people, Mackenzie and other
Patriot refugees were also staying. Judge Jones posed as a gentleman from Kingston, Head as his valet. He was recognized, of
course, but treated with great courtesy by the rebel leaders, and
finally left the hotel in a coach and four with the Patriots cheering him on his way.

The evening before his departure, the Governor had invited
FitzGibbon to dine with him. Sir Francis had done a complete
about-face, joining the citizens of Toronto in lauding and ap-
plauding the success of FitzGibbon. But once Sir Francis reached
England, he changed his tune and filled his *Narrative* with er-
rors or lies that discredited FitzGibbon. The citizens of Toronto
greeted the publication with angry protest and called a public
meeting on the subject.

As early as January, the House of Assembly had passed resolutions to reward Fitz for saving the city and possibly also the province. "Resolved, — That this House do humbly address Her Majesty, praying Her Majesty will be graciously pleased to grant to the said James FitzGibbon five thousand acres of the waste lands of the Crown in this province."

FitzGibbon's spirits rose to a new height. The debt that had oppressed him all his life could be lifted from his head. His wife and children could have the prosperity he wanted for them. From being treated as a public nuisance by Head he would now be officially honoured. But this reward, and others, were to be dangled before him the rest of his life, and he would never receive any land. Allan MacNab, who lived in debt on a much grander scale in his Dundurn Castle at Burlington Heights, at least received a knighthood from Her Majesty and a sword from the colonists. It took Fitz ten years to receive a grant of money and the frustration he felt ruined his health.

In June 1838, Fitz learned that the request by the Legislative Council and Assembly to reward him had been turned down in London. What happened was that the same Legislature had passed an act to put an end to the promiscuous granting of lands. Thus Her Majesty could not reasonably make a grant of land to FitzGibbon. Friends urged Fitz to go to London to plead his case. He spent six months there but gained nothing. Meanwhile, the matter kept coming up in the Legislature at home but nothing was achieved.

Mary died on March 22, 1841, and was buried beside her brother-in-law, Simon Washburn, in St. James churchyard. It was 1845 before Parliament finally voted Fitz £1,000 instead of the land. He used it to pay off a number of his debts. But it had come too late to save his health. Constant financial anxiety coupled with worry over Mary who had never really been well since the tragic death of their son, George, had worn away at the old Green Tiger's spirit.

After Mary's death Fitz followed the government to Kingston. In the Union Act of 1840, the British Parliament had created a single Province of Canada uniting Upper and Lower Canada. In an effort to provide a central location, the new compromise capital was Kingston. Fitz kept the Toronto house, knowing it would increase in value, but paying high interest to hold onto it. Only five acres of the original eighteen now remained free from mortgage.

When the government was to move to Montreal, FitzGibbon was unable to go. He handed in his resignation in May 1846, with a certificate from Dr. Widmer stating that he was no longer able to serve as clerk of the House. The letter with which Dr. Widmer accompanied this certificate drew a tragic picture of the one-time hero of Beaver Dam, now a victim not only of his own nature but of the times he lived in, caught between the tides of reaction and reform.

> It is now thirty years since I became acquainted with Captain FitzGibbon, then in the Glengarry Light Infantry. The war with America had then just concluded, and the whole community of Upper Canada, civil and military, was full of applause in regard to the conduct of Captain FitzGibbon, during the course of the preceding campaigns.
>
> It was justly pronounced that his services had been of the highest order, and contributed to stamp his corps with the character of vigour, vigilance and valour.
>
> During a long series of years of peace, the same qualities which rendered him conspicuous as a military man, were productive of an effective and highly honourable discharge of the duties of the offices he held in civil life.
>
> And thus would the useful and faithful course of Captain FitzGibbon's career have terminated in civil engagements, but for the occurrence of the unnatural attempt of the rebels to sever the country from British connection, in 1837. At this crisis the foresight and energy of Captain Fitz-Gibbon saved the city of Toronto from destruction, and were the means of shortening a struggle that might otherwise have been protracted. For these services alone, the gratitude of the Government is eminently due to Captain FitzGibbon. His expectations of a release from pecuniary embarrassments have been raised by a vote of the Legislature for a grant of land grounded on the high value at

which it estimated his services during the rebellion. These expectations having failed in their accomplishment, to my knowledge, has had a powerful effect in destroying the healthy tone of his mind, and has rendered him incapable of performing the active duties of his office, and almost unfitted him for the social intercourse of his friends and acquaintances.

(Signed) C. Widmer.

But there was fight left in the old Green Tiger yet. His second son, William, was clerk of the County of Hastings and his residence in Belleville became home to Fitz while he recovered. If his mind was in a poor confused condition in these days, he took care that his body kept in good condition. He had always been a great believer in exercise. Mary Agnes FitzGibbon wrote:

The spectacle of a man turned of sixty-five years of age, clad in jerseys, swinging himself from a bar fixed across the supports of the verandah, doubling himself up into a ball, jumping through his hands, or hanging by his feet, drawing his body up by sheer strength of muscle, and anon leaping over chairs arranged in rows, was quite sufficient to obtain him a certificate of insanity from the majority of his neighbours.

The fact that he particularly liked to exercise on bright moonlight nights in summer, made his performance an even greater curiosity.

By the beginning of 1847, FitzGibbon felt well enough to go to England. A friend, Charles Mackay, wrote of him, "living for six months in London on sixpence a day, fourpence of which was spent in bread, one penny for milk, and the remaining penny for sugar, and assuring him [Mackay] that he never felt so well in his life."

What happened was that Fitz had gone abroad in June expecting that by the end of July he would receive the first installment of a pension of £300 a year, granted to him on retirement in 1846. Its late arrival left him living on sixpence a day.

During these years he made many new friends, among these

the Strickland sisters, Elizabeth and Jane. Back in Canada, Fitz-Gibbon's son, Charles, had become engaged to their niece, Agnes, daughter of Susanna Strickland Moodie. Fitz went often to the cottage in Bayswater where Elizabeth lived, and the letters they exchanged show that they were very fond of one another.

In 1850 FitzGibbon was appointed one of the Military Knights of Windsor. The order had been founded in the fourteenth century for the support of twenty-four soldiers "who had distinguished themselves in the wars, and had afterwards been reduced to straits." He would live within the walls of Windsor Castle, opposite St. George's Chapel, would receive a small salary and be required to attend services at St. George's.

Here his final years were passed in congenial company, sharing with the other knights a lively interest in worldly affairs both present and past. The first years were not easy for again he was almost starving so that he could pay off debts, determined that he would die owing to no man. His brother Gerald in Ireland had lent him £1,000 in 1841 and when all his other debts were paid and only £60 owing to Gerald, his brother dismissed the debt so that James could live out a little of his life free from worry.

By far the happiest days now were when a friend from the far distant past came to visit him. An old comrade who had been with him under Nelson at Copenhagen ended a letter to say he was coming like this, "As I intend, in the course of a short time, to clinch the tow-rope of pleasure by hailing your snuggery at Windsor Castle, I therefore cut my pen yarn short, and will spin one as long as the main top bowling when we meet to talk in good earnest, and fight our battles of glorious record o'er and o'er again."

His association with the family of Sir Isaac Brock lasted all his life. The intense hero worship which he felt for Brock, and which had set the course of his life, stayed with him always. In a letter written late in life he refers to the Battle of Beaver Dam:

> When I brought in those five hundred prisoners and delivered them up to General Vincent, I then thought I would have given the world's wealth to have General Brock there

alive to say to him, "Here, sir, is the first installment of my debt of gratitude to you for all you have done for me. In words I have never thanked you, because words could never express my gratitude for such generous protection as you have hitherto unceasingly extended to me."

Another letter which speaks of Isaac Brock as his earliest and best benefactor adds, "And if there was another man for whom I felt an almost equal degree of regard and gratitude, that man was John Savery Brock. I am indulging the hope of one day seeing his widow and children in Guernsey." Savery was Brock's younger brother who had been dismissed from the navy for objecting to the cruel punishment meted out to sailors. He had served with Isaac's regiment as paymaster for about six years. Fitz would always remember him as the man running ahead of the soldiers from one sandhill to another at Egmont-op-Zee; his survival that day convinced FitzGibbon that out in front was the best place to be in any attack.

There is no account of FitzGibbon actually visiting the Isle of Guernsey. It is more than likely that his determination to pay off debts made it impossible for him ever to see the birthplace of the Brocks.

James died on December 10, 1863. He was eighty-three years old. His children, William, Mary, and James had died in the 1850's; only Charles survived him.

In his last few years he had longed to come home to Canada. In 1855 he wrote to Walter Mackenzie, one of the young lads he had drilled in military tactics in the 1830's: "I sometimes exclaim, 'Thank God, I have Canada to fall back upon.' Its future seems to me more full of promise than that of any other section of the human family. I long to be among you."

In his last year, when almost unable to leave his bed, he questioned his doctor about the possibility of an ocean voyage home. There he could lie by his wife Mary, in the churchyard of St. James in Toronto. But instead he was to die in London and lie in the catacombs of St. George's Cathedral, a long way from Niagara where the Green Tiger had fought so well in the war, a long way from Toronto where the public servant had fought the longer, devastating battles of the peace.

References

Cruikshank, Lt.-Col. E. *The Documentary History of the Campaign on the Niagara Frontier.* Welland, Ont.: Tribune Office, n.d.

Dunlop, Dr. Wm. *Recollections of the War of 1812.* Toronto: Historical Publishing Co., 1908.

Edgar, Lady Matilda. *General Brock.* Toronto: Morang & Co. Ltd., 1910.

—— *Ten Years of Upper Canada in Peace and War: 1805-15.* Toronto: William Briggs, 1890.

FitzGibbon, Mary Agnes. *A Veteran of 1812.* Toronto: William Briggs, 1894.

Guillet, Edwin C. *Lives and Times of the Patriots.* Toronto: The Ontario Publishing Company Ltd., 1838.

Hanney, James. *A History of the War of 1812.* Toronto: Morang & Co. Ltd., 1905.

Hitsman, J. MacKay. *The Incredible War of 1812.* Toronto: University of Toronto Press, 1965.

Jameson, Mrs. Anna. *Winter Studies and Summer Rambles in Canada.* London: Saunders and Otley, 1838.

Mackenzie, Ruth. *Laura Secord: The Legend and the Lady.* Toronto: McClelland and Stewart, 1971.

Nursey, W.R. *The Story of Isaac Brock*. Toronto: William Briggs, 1909.

Read, D.B. *Life and Times of Major General Sir Issac Brock*. Toronto: William Briggs, 1894.

The Story of Laura Ingersoll Secord. Ontario Department of Public Records and Archives, Misc.: 1933.